Blair Worden, recently recognised by *BBC History Magazine* as 'the pre-eminent historian of Cromwellian England', has taught at the universities of Cambridge, Oxford, Sussex and Chicago, and is now Research Professor of History at Royal Holloway College London. He is a Fellow of the British Academy and has been Literary Director of the Royal Historical Society. He has written widely on the political, intellectual and religious history of early modern England. His publications on the civil wars include *The Rump Parliament 1648–1653; Roundhead Reputations; The English Civil Wars and the Passions of Posterity;* and most recently *Literature and Politics in Cromwellian England.*

By Blair Worden

The Rump Parliament 1648–1653

The Sound of Virtue: Philip Sidney's 'Arcadia'
and Elizabethan Politics

Roundhead Reputations: The English Civil Wars
and Passions of Posterity

Literature and Politics in Cromwellian England:
John Milton, Andrew Marvell, Marchamont Needham

The English Civil Wars 1640–1660

THE ENGLISH CIVIL WARS
1640–1660

➤✦◄

BLAIR WORDEN

PHOENIX

A PHOENIX PAPERBACK

First published in Great Britain in 2009
by Weidenfeld & Nicolson
This paperback edition published in 2009
by Phoenix,
an imprint of Orion Books Ltd,
Orion House, 5 Upper St Martin's Lane,
London, WC2H 9EA

An Hachette UK company

7 9 10 8

Copyright © Blair Worden 2009

A CIP catalogue record for this book
is available from the British Library.

ISBN 978-0-7538-2691-1

Typeset by Input Data Services Ltd,
Bridgwater, Somerset

Printed and bound by CPI Group
(UK) Ltd, Croydon, CR0 4YY

The Orion Publishing Group's policy is to use papers
that are natural, renewable and recyclable products and
made from wood grown in sustainable forests. The logging
and manufacturing processes are expected to conform to
the environmental regulations of the country of origin.

www.orionbooks.co.uk

For Richard, Jenny and Hugo Davenport-Hines
and in memory of Cosmo Davenport-Hines 1986–2008

CONTENTS

PREFACE

❖·❖

Professional historians nowadays delight in the complexity and density of the subject to which this book offers an introduction. Readers outside the world of specialized academic study can consequently find its outlines elusive. I mean my account to be as straightforward as is compatible with adult discussion and with the picture which modern research has produced. Though it draws pervasively on the work of others, I hope that it brings some fresh findings and perspectives. One word is needed about terminology. 'The civil war' will mean the war fought between king and parliament in 1642–6. 'The civil wars' will mean the range of conflicts, military and political, of the 1640s and 1650s.

I

ORIGINS

❧⭒❧

The political upheaval of the mid-seventeenth century has no parallel in English history. Since the Norman Conquest there have been other forcible convulsions: the baronial revolts and Wars of the Roses of the middle ages; the religious and regional risings of the Tudor age; the 'Glorious Revolution' of 1688–9. But none has been so far-reaching, or has disrupted so many lives for so long, or has so imprinted itself on the nation's memory.

Sometimes such other events have changed the occupancy or the powers of the throne, but the conflict of 1640–60 was more extensive. The monarchy and the House of Lords were abolished, and were replaced by a republic and military rule. The government and liturgy of the Church of England were abolished too. England has been set apart from other European nations, especially in modern times, by its ancient and unwritten constitution, an amalgam of evolving law and custom. Yet the mid-seventeenth century ruptured that continuity and brought, under the protectorate of Oliver Cromwell, two written constitutions.

If there has been no event like it, none has so divided posterity. Even to choose a term for the episode is to risk disagreement. From the Restoration to the nineteenth century, when royalist and Tory perspectives dominated, the common phrase was 'the rebellion' or 'the great rebellion', while allusions to the 'troubles' or 'distractions' of the period were also common. More subtly the same perspective produced the phrase 'The Interregnum' to represent Puritan rule as a deviation from the healthy norm of kingship, though that term has lost its partisan intent.

Since the Victorian age, when the balance of public sympathy swung from the king's cause to parliament's, an alternative vocabulary has flourished. It presents the wars, not as an aberration, but as a stage in the country's progress, even the world's progress, towards the present. Nineteenth-century writers found in the political demands of the king's opponents a foretaste of Victorian constitutional arrangements. Likewise admiring the parliamentarians' spiritual earnestness, they called the episode 'the Puritan Revolution'. In the twentieth century, when more secular outlooks prevailed, the term 'the English Revolution' cast it as the first modern revolution, the precursor of the French and Russian Revolutions.

Perhaps 'the English civil wars', having neither a derogatory nor a commendatory flavour, is as near to neutrality as we can get. Some historians would now prefer 'the British civil wars'. Regretting the Anglocentricity that permeated the study of British history during the twentieth century, they seek, in the spirit of an age of devolution, to make amends. The term usefully emphasizes the interaction of English events with the contemporary upheavals in Ireland, then effectively a colony, and Scotland, then a foreign country. But it also risks exaggerating it, and can obscure the distinctiveness of each of the three conflicts.

Although the Irish and Scottish wars broke less constitutional or ideological ground than England's, present-day investigation is revealing the wealth and width of interest that those other conflicts might command if historians of Ireland and Scotland were to bring them alive for a general readership. But that is a challenge for other books. In this one, Irish and Scottish events figure as contributors to the English struggle.

Why did the English civil wars happen? On the face of it, the country should have been less vulnerable to political breakdown under the Stuart dynasty, which succeeded in 1603, than under the Tudors before it. In the sixteenth century the transformation of religious belief and social practice by the Reformation had wrought havoc on the Continent. The protracted religious wars of France and the Netherlands in the later part of the century frequently threatened to spread to England, probably through a combination of native rebellion and invasion by one of the great Catholic powers: Spain, with which England was at war from 1585, and France. Even if Queen Elizabeth were to withstand those disasters, her failure to produce an heir or settle the succession appeared to doom England to them on her death.

The smooth succession of James VI of Scotland as James I of England produced surprise and relief. He brought advantages which Elizabeth had lacked. He had sons, so that there need be no succession problem for long to come. Scotland had been the 'back door' through which Continental powers had hoped to enter England. Now that the two countries shared a dynasty, the door was closed. In any case the Continental wars wound down around the turn of the century, and in 1604 James made peace with Spain. There would be renewed Continental warfare from 1618, when the Thirty Years War began, but the joint prospect of conquest and revolt was never as imminent under James or his son Charles as before them.

Other developments appeared to aid rather than threaten domestic stability. The Tudors had nationalized the Church and made it officially Protestant, but the conversion of the population to the new faith had been a slow and painful process. By the reign of James I, while far from complete, it was well advanced, and for the time being Protestantism did more to unite England than divide it. Gradually, too, the Tudors had tamed the magnates whose powers had undermined or restricted medieval kingship. The north, where both aristocratic defiance and Catholic belief posed their largest dangers, was brought to order.

More peaceable times produced more peaceable thinking. Under the Tudors, both Protestant and Catholic dissidents had alarmed their rulers by invoking the right or duty of subjects to rise against tyrannical or ungodly princes. If the Elizabethan regime had broken down, say, around 1580, a likely enough prospect at the time, much would have been heard of that adventurous argument. Not much would be heard of it in the lead-up to the civil wars, when parliament, no less than the crown, saw itself as the preserver of tradition and of established law, and portrayed its adversary as the innovator in both Church and state. No one foresaw the chaos of the ensuing two decades, which produced events and ideas far distant from, and far disproportionate to, the initial aims of the participants. There is no better illustration of the law of unintended consequences than the English civil wars.

Admittedly England, and Britain, were far from alone in

experiencing civil strife in the mid-seventeenth century. Portugal, Catalonia and Naples rose against the government of Madrid. France was crippled by the aristocratic and constitutional rebellions of the Frondes. There were political upheavals in Sweden, Denmark and the Netherlands. 'These days', observed a preacher to the English House of Commons in 1643, 'are days of shaking', 'and this shaking is universal: the Palatinate, Bohemia, Germany, Catalonia, Portugal, Ireland, England'.

Yet the Continental revolts were less extensive, both in their effects and in their ideas, than the English wars. They arose from the financial and social strains of the Thirty Years War, that monumental struggle from which England, except for a brief period in the 1620s, kept clear. Though the European conflict had begun as a clash of religion, it had been largely shorn of that dimension by the 1640s, when the struggle had become one for military supremacy between the great Catholic powers. By contrast England, which had hitherto escaped religious warfare, now succumbed to it.

In November 1641, when the parliament which would go to war with the king had been sitting for a year, the House of Commons passed a 'remonstrance of the state of the kingdom', 'the Grand Remonstrance' as it would come to be called, which it soon published as a rallying call to the nation. It lists the deeds of misgovernment with which parliament and the nation have had to contend.

The long catalogue starts at 'the beginning of His Majesty's reign', in 1625, when Charles was aged twenty-four. The king himself is not blamed for them. At this stage the conventions of deference still persuaded MPs to attribute misrule to evil advisers and conspirators around the monarch. Yet the document leaves no doubt that the country's problems have arisen from his reign. It objects, not to the rights and powers of kingship, but to what has happened under a single king. In all the legislative initiatives pursued by the parliament before the war, and in all its negotiations with the king during and after it, there is never a hint that England's constitution or form of government is flawed. The difficulty was to disempower Charles I while preserving the nation's ancient laws and customs.

Can the civil wars really be ascribed to the defects of the king? To a modern reader, accustomed perhaps to structural or sociological explanations of great events, the suggestion may sound trivializing. It is indeed insufficient. Many of the provocative things that Charles I said and did about parliaments and Puritans have parallels in the reign of his father and even of the Tudors. He faced challenges that would have taxed any ruler. The relations of executive and legislature, and the threats to the state's solvency on which they turned, were an enduring seventeenth-century problem, as contentious under Oliver Cromwell, and then under the restored monarchy, as before the civil wars.

Besides, Charles was a dutiful king who, at least by his own lights, clung to virtues of honour and conscience. He aimed at standards of public probity. He put an end to the moral laxity at court that had given offence under James. He effected overdue administrative reforms – even if one result of his naval and military changes was to equip ships and soldiers that would soon fight against him, and even if his attempts to standardize local administration antagonized JPs and other rulers of the shires who were used to running things their way. Personally he could be charming and considerate. He could be an effective leader of his supporters and was brave in battle.

Unfortunately he brought to his rule three qualities which, though none of them need have been disastrous on its own, were fatal in combination. First, he had alarming policies, which he pursued with alarming methods. Secondly he was incorrigibly deficient in political judgement. Whether or not his goals were attainable, they required realistic assessments of the balance of political power, and of the likely consequences of his actions, that were too often beyond him. Thirdly no one could trust him. Behind his duplicity there lay failings of political imagination and of personal presence and authority. His goals required arts of management and persuasion to which he was again unequal, largely because of an inability to enter the minds of people with views different from his own or to take sensitive or tactful account of their concerns. An inner insecurity made him wary of public display and denied him regality of manner. He sought self-certainty through a ruthless determination to be obeyed. When he bargained or compromised, it was only while secretly plotting the destruction of those with whom he negotiated. More often than not the secret leaked.

Those who opposed him in the 1640s believed themselves to be contending on two fronts: for 'the liberty of the subject', which depended on the free meetings and debates of parliaments and on the security of property, and for 'religion'. The relationship between the two causes exercised the participants and has puzzled posterity. In 1672 the poet and polemicist Andrew Marvell, looking back on the turmoil of the mid-century, would grasp the folly of asking 'whether it were a war of religion, or of liberty', for 'whichsoever was at the top, the other was at the bottom'. Wars are never fought for religion alone. What we call the 'wars of religion' in sixteenth- and seventeenth-century Europe were conducted between rival faiths, but also between crown and nobility or between one nation or principality and another. It was the conjuncture of religious and political conflict that destroyed Charles I. Both had long roots, but it was Charles whose words and deeds brought them together.

England's civil wars, though a number of Catholics enlisted in them, were fought between alternative visions of the Protestant faith. In European terms the Church of England that emerged from the Reformation was an eccentric creation. There were two main strands to the Continental Reformation: the Lutheran one, which began the movement, and the more militantly organized Swiss one, which was largely controlled by John Calvin from Geneva. In doctrines of faith, England followed the Swiss model. But in France and the Netherlands, as also in Scotland, Calvinism won power or influence from below, through revolt. England's Reformation was imposed from on high, by its rulers, a practice characteristically Lutheran rather than Calvinist. Continental Calvinists had rejected the hierarchical structure of medieval Church government. They replaced episcopacy (the rule of bishops), which ruled the parishes from above, by presbyteries, whose authority rested on the local participation of believers. But the English monarchy, which made use of the bishops to control the Church, preserved the Catholic structure even as it absorbed Calvinist theology.

Under Elizabeth that hybrid organization, or halfway house, struggled for a sense of identity. How could it vindicate itself against the growing confidence of Counter-Reformation Catholicism on the one hand, and native pressure for Presbyterian change on the other? Yet by James's reign the Church of England had found its confidence. Had not the very moderation of the English Reformation, its adoption of a middle way, spared the country the fanaticism and destruction of the Continent's religious wars? Under James the episcopal structure was barely challenged. Yet there were tensions. Two rival perspectives emerged, which under his shrewd management coexisted and often over-lapped, but which under Charles would divide and then break the nation. For shorthand, greatly as it simplifies, we can call them Puritan and Anglican.

'Puritanism' was a derogatory term. Those who found themselves subjected to it preferred to think of themselves as 'the godly', though bolder spirits among them preferred 'the saints'. Yet the hostile term usefully encapsulates a movement. The central positions of Puritanism were defined and hardened only after long debate, and even then were recurrently challenged on the periphery. Here we concentrate on the mainstream. If the movement has a single origin it lies in the translations of the Bible into English that were made during and after the Reformation. They were a trans-forming development in English thought and culture. For Puritans, and not for them alone, they made God's word the first guide to all experience, worldly and spiritual. Readers met a God of two faces: the Old Testament God, the maker and breaker of nations, implacable in his justice, vengeful in the punishment of his earthly adversaries and betrayers; and the New Testament God of mercy, whose gift of salvation brings the waters of divine grace to the barren or afflicted soul.

Through Puritan endeavour there ran an evangelical instinct: the zeal to promote, by preaching and reading, the Gospel truths which bring salvation. Puritans were repelled by the obstacles to that advance: by worldly vanities and sensual delights which distract or destroy the soul; and by display and ceremony in worship, which substitute formality for the life of the spirit, images for the word of God, idolatry for faith. They insisted on the strict observation of the Sabbath. Eager to legislate for the worship of their neighbours, they imposed rigorous spiritual regimes on themselves. In private meditations, or in consultation with each other, they scrutinized God's 'providences', his startling interventions in public and private life. Those happenings prompted them to the alternately joyous and anguished self-examination which, in their theological scheme, awakens the believer's soul, turns it against sin, and guides it to sanctification and to union with Christ.

Puritans tended to be millenarians, that is, interpreters of current conflicts as evidence of the decay of the world and as harbingers of Christ's kingdom (though the boldest millenarian theories, which predicted the date of the Second Coming, were confined to a small minority). And they subscribed to the theory that the modern imagination perhaps finds the hardest of their beliefs to enter: the doctrine of predestination, the divine decree which from eternity dooms most of depraved humanity to damnation, but which exempts the elect few to whom, through God's inexplicable mercy and through no merits or exertions of their own, divine grace and a heavenly future are imparted.

Though there was much in those positions that was shared with other religious parties, Puritanism gave them intense forms. The doctrine of predestination was broadly accepted by the late Elizabethan and the Jacobean Church leadership, but largely as an intellectual proposition: as a standpoint from which to refute the Catholic assertion that men could be saved by good works. In the Puritan scheme, where the believer, on the path to assurance of election, wrestles alone before God with the consciousness and temptations of sin, the doctrine was the kernel of spiritual life.

Yet by James's reign the intellectual foundations of predestination were under threat from the Anglican tendency. Ideologies have a way of establishing themselves by uncompromising confrontation with old beliefs, but then, in ensuing generations, of consolidating their public impact by self-modification and by compromise with humanity's imperfections – to the dismay of the harder ideologues, who cling to their original doctrine. So it was with Calvinism. Suggestions grew, especially among younger men, that Calvin's denial of free will was an affront to God, whom it makes a tyrant; and that even if the human capacity for reason and virtue and reverence, corrupted as it had been by the Fall, could not earn salvation alone, it might turn the soul towards divine grace and so hope to meet it.

The same trend affected attitudes to the practices of worship. To Puritans, the Reformation had not gone far enough. To Anglicans it had gone, or threatened to go, too far. In their eyes the break with Rome was, or ought to have been, not a repudiation of tradition but the recovery of ancient native practices: the restoration, as it were, of a beautiful but long-neglected garden. Anglicans did repudiate the papal supremacy and such cardinal points of Catholicism as the Latin liturgy and Latin Bible, the celibacy of the clergy, and the doctrine of transubstantiation. But they believed the establishment of papal control in the middle ages to have been a usurpation and corruption of an English Church which had its own venerable heritage.

The present persuasive power of the Church, they maintained, lay not in sermons, on which Puritans laid too much stress, but in the comely observation of the sacraments, in set forms of prayer and worship, and in the affirmations and solaces and verbal rhythms of the Prayer Book, which placed the rituals of birth, marriage and death in the great and essentially unaltering continuum of time. Where Puritans tended to think of church buildings as mere venues, the plainer the better, for the gathering of believers, and frequently took little care for their upkeep, Anglicans set store by their appearance to the outward eye. Some of them also fretted to remember the obliteration of that prominent link with the medieval past, the monasteries, and to recall the acquisition of monastic lands, and of the church livings that belonged to them, by lay families which too often put their own profits before the service of God.

Charles I came to the throne in the middle of a calamitous decade for European Protestantism, which banished the sense of relative international relaxation that, despite occasional scares, had grown up around the Jacobean court. In 1620–3 James's Protestant son-in-law the Elector Palatine, the Rhineland prince on whose contest with his Catholic neighbours the European struggle between the two faiths had come to focus, was ignominiously deprived of his territories by troops of the Habsburgs, the dynastic line shared by the kings of Spain with the Holy Roman emperors who ruled lands of and to the east and south-east of Germany. In the ensuing years Catholic armies swept into northern Europe.

The proper place of religion in English foreign policy was a divisive issue, with which the debate on the future of the English Church was embroiled. Puritans wanted to be loyal to both their faith and their country, but a number of them were ready, if their country should betray their faith, to live or fight overseas on religion's behalf. To them the purpose of diplomacy was to aid their threatened or persecuted co-religionists abroad. To Anglicans, who were fonder of the differences than of the similarities between English and Continental Protestantism, that view seemed fanatical. It found equally little favour with more pragmatic thinkers, who sought to separate foreign policy from religion. They argued that the nation, instead of incurring the costs and risks of a crusade, should live on peaceful terms with the Habsburgs and tackle the challenge posed to England's prosperity by that economic miracle of the seventeenth century, the wealth achieved by the Protestant Dutch through their maritime carrying trade and their exploitation of new colonial markets.

That England had an obligation to help the Elector Palatine regain his throne was common ground between the crown and Puritanism. But whereas the crown, which saw his disgrace as a dynastic rather than a religious disaster, strove to reverse it through friendship with Madrid, Puritans favoured a resumption of the Elizabethan naval war and an assault on Spanish possessions in the Caribbean. Both were fanciful ambitions, which exaggerated the pressure that

England could exert on a much greater power. The plight of Continental Protestantism, and the grim public mood that it induced, pervaded England's political conflicts of the 1620s. Even in the brief period, at the end of James's reign and the beginning of Charles's, when the crown did enter the Continental conflict, a combination of diplomatic and military bungling led to the humiliation of forces sent to the coasts of Holland, France and Spain. Failure abroad wrought damage at home. The two eras of crisis in Charles's relations with parliament, the first in 1626–9, the second in 1640–2, both had as their background the nation's wretched defeat in war.

What prompted those crises? One might expect England, a small country, to have been relatively easy to govern. The Norman Conquest, and the judicial and administrative systems that were built in its wake, had given the monarchy a measure of control over the whole country and had established uniform institutions of rule (though Wales was only assimilated under Henry VIII). By contrast kings in Paris and Madrid had had to annex their outlying territories and to contend with the rights and autonomous instincts of distant provinces. Facing larger challenges, the Continental rulers of the sixteenth and seventeenth centuries took larger steps. They built up standing armies and bureaucracies, and weakened the estates and representative institutions that obstructed them.

The English monarchy was less ambitious. Its power, military and political, rested on the voluntary cooperation of its subjects, and especially of the substantial landowners in whose hands the supervision of local government predominantly lay. In normal times their consent was readily forthcoming. Habits of conformity and obedience ran deep in a society which agreed that tyranny, however hideous, was preferable to anarchy, an assumption that indicates the desperation that in 1642 led parliament to risk the chaos of civil war. Besides, the local standing of landowners, and their chances of office or favour at court, depended on royal approval, or else on the backing of magnates who were themselves dependent on it. Over the sixteenth and early seventeenth centuries, when the scope of local administration greatly expanded, the gentry educated themselves, at universities and the inns of court and through private study, to run it. The same training prepared them to compete for office at Whitehall.

Yet it also equipped them, should consensus break down, to make trouble: not through armed resistance, which from James's accession until the breakdown of Charles I's rule seemed a thing of the past, but through civilian means, and especially in parliament. From the late sixteenth century the crown sensed a weakening of its position. The gentry, together with the population at large, were increasing in number; so was the composition of the House of Commons; and the greater the number of candidates for office and favour, the smaller the proportion whom the crown had the resources to reward. The language grew up of 'court' and 'country', which idealized the plain virtues, and the independence of mind, of 'patriots' who put the good of the community before the sectional interests of courtiers. It also offered a consoling perspective to unsuccessful competitors in the scramble for office.

Politics turned largely on interpretations of the law, a subject on which landowners, themselves increasingly litigious in their property disputes, were acquiring expertise. In the generations before the civil wars there grew a reverence for the common law as, among other virtues, a guarantor of political liberty. A heightening and broadening of political awareness is visible on other fronts too: in the growing quantity of the documents – official compilations, and private diaries and correspondence – that recorded political events; in the readiness of MPs, in a society that put a high value on the authority of the past, to encourage research into medieval political precedents and to cite the results for partisan purposes; and in a hunger for political information, which by the 1620s was being satisfied by the distribution of newsletters from London to the shires. Political alertness was not confined to the owners of estates. It extended to merchants, to lawyers, and to the constables and other local enforcers of law or policy on whose cooperation the crown was again dependent.

In the early Stuart age, as in every other, political principles were fuelled and exploited by self-interest and by the competition for power. National or local ties of kinship or patronage, and ancient rivalries between families, mingled with and shaped issues of public policy. But they did not manufacture them. The issues were debated in the royal court and council; in the law courts at Westminster; in the local assizes and the meetings of gentry as local governors; and in elections to parliament.

Parliaments were occasional bodies, which met only at the crown's bidding and were dissolved at its will. Their customary tasks were to vote taxes, to vet or propose legislation, and to offer deferential advice to the crown. They were caught between pressures from above, where royal councillors in both Lords and Commons sought to steer the debates, and from below, from the constituents to whom members of the Commons were answerable, and who liked to demand that the grievances of the subject be redressed before revenue were granted. Although most MPs were chosen through agreement among the local gentry, or, in towns, among a coterie of the principal citizens, there were constituencies where contested elections, and erratic franchise regulations, produced a much wider participation. Here too the crown, which looked to powerful courtiers to manage elections, sensed its authority slipping away.

Within parliament, however, it was that institution's own authority that seemed in jeopardy. Would not parliament go the way of its Continental counterparts? 'This is the crisis of parliaments,' declared one MP in a political emergency in 1628. 'We shall know by this if parliaments live or die.' In the event they lived, because of their social strength. Where the kings of France and Spain set the estates, and the classes they represented, against each other, in England there were no classes to divide. Lords and Commons were separate political orders but not separate economic or political interests. The system of primogeniture, which passed property to the firstborn male, and required his brothers to seek incomes elsewhere, produced intermarriage and social fluidity between peers and gentry, and between gentry and lawyers or merchants or aldermen. Parliaments could speak, if not for the whole nation, then at least for its political heart.

One problem neither they nor the monarchy could solve: the insufficiency of the crown's revenue as a result of its failure to keep pace with a long period of high inflation. The collection of parliamentary taxes, which were anyway unrealistically low, encountered effective foot-dragging in the localities. Unable to pay its ministers and civil servants with proper salaries, the crown rewarded them with perks and with financial or trading concessions, such as monopolies of the sale of goods, which appeared to damage the economy. A remnant of feudal law entitled the state, through the Court of Wards, to annex and sell the wardship of heirs whose fathers had died before the wards themselves had reached adulthood.

The crown's fiscal expedients left a stain of corruption and provoked a resentment that was enhanced by the extravagance and opulence which, to the dismay of 'the country', characterized the royal entourage of the early seventeenth century, as it did the courts of the Continent. The government's debts soared in wartime, for recent changes in the conduct of warfare had swollen the size and costs of armies and campaigns. MPs were readier to vote for war than to oblige their constituents to pay for it, a tendency that exasperated Charles I early in his reign, when he briefly committed himself to the aggressive foreign policy which MPs demanded but was denied by them the means to finance it.

The monarchy's inevitable response to parliamentary parsimony was to look to non-parliamentary taxes and to seek to establish their legality. James I succeeded in increasing the customs rates, a major source of royal revenue, without parliamentary sanction. Charles, early in his reign, levied first a 'benevolence' and then, more successfully, a 'loan', which no one expected to be repaid. Some recent historians have played down the consequent constitutional crisis and similar conflicts of the later 1620s, but neither their gravity nor their significance will go away. In 1627 the political temperature rose when five knights who had refused the loan were imprisoned by royal command, and failed to secure release after suing a Habeas Corpus.

In the first four years of his reign Charles called three parliaments, a high rate of frequency. All of them ended in acrimony. Pleas by MPs and others for the rule of law and the rights of property became increasingly anxious. The king justified the loan by invoking the crown's entitlement to raise money in what it deemed an emergency. Arguably his obligation to aid his beleaguered uncle Christian IV of Denmark after his defeat by Habsburg forces in 1626 constituted one, but Charles's constitutional thinking extended beyond that crisis. Unless parliaments came to heel, he warned, he would adopt 'new counsels', by which he meant the non-parliamentary methods of his neighbour kings.

Parliament asserted the nation's liberties in the Petition of Right, which it presented to the king in 1628. MPs speaking in its support warned of the danger to the 'birthright and inheritance' of Englishmen posed by the claim, which threatened to make his subjects 'slaves', that he possessed 'a sovereign power ... above the laws and statutes of this kingdom'. Neither Charles's ostensible acceptance of the Petition, which he subsequently bypassed, nor the assassination later in the year of his hated favourite the Duke of Buckingham, on whom much of the blame for recent policies and disasters had been laid, could assuage the public fears. In 1629 a group of MPs, defying the king's order for the adjournment of parliament, held the Speaker of the Commons in his chair while the House passed resolutions declaring anyone who aided the crown's circumvention of parliament to be 'a capital enemy to this kingdom'.

It was an extremist statement, which played into the king's hands, but the extremism was born of despair. Charles dissolved the parliament, had the ringleaders tried and imprisoned, and announced an end to parliaments until his people had 'come to a better understanding of themselves'. Only eleven years later, when duress had eliminated all other options, would he call another.

The parliamentary resolutions of 1629 proscribed another category of 'capital enemy': 'whosoever shall bring in an innovation of religion or by favour or countenance seek to extend or introduce popery or Arminianism, or other opinion disagreeing from the true and orthodox Church'. The noun 'Arminianism' alluded to Calvin's critic the Dutch divine Jacobus Arminius, who had caused uproar in the Netherlands by repudiating the doctrine of predestination, though the word came to be used loosely, as it will be here, to signify the Anglican tendency. 'Popery', a looser term still, is one of the dominant concepts of seventeenth-century politics. The nation's identity had become bound to the defence of Protestantism against the external threat from Catholic powers and from the papacy, which had excommunicated Queen Elizabeth and had incited murderous conspiracy against her. It was bound, too, to landmark memories: the persecution and burnings of Protestants by Queen Mary, and those astonishing deliverances at God's hands, the defeat of the Spanish Armada in 1588 and the thwarting of the Gunpowder Plot in 1605.

Most English Catholics were faithful to the crown, from which they hoped for toleration as a reward for their loyalty, but their submissiveness did not abate the alarm at the apparent growth in their numbers in the early seventeenth century and at what Protestants called the 'swarm' of foreign priests and Jesuits who slipped invisibly into England. The fear of 'popish' conspiracy would animate, and be exploited by, the parliamentary leadership of 1640–2; it would produce the hysteria surrounding the alleged 'popish plot' of 1678 and the subsequent moves to exclude the Catholic heir, the future James II, from the throne; and it would bring James himself down in 1688. The Puritan vision of a godly commonwealth was always a minority viewpoint, but the Puritan hatred of popery, being a patriotic as well as a spiritual sentiment, had a broad rallying power.

Yet 'popery' meant different things to different people. To Arminians it merely alluded to the ambitions of the papacy and its following. In Puritan minds popery was infiltrating, in Charles I's reign, the Church of England itself. It was present in its ceremonialism and in the advances of the doctrine of free will. As the Catholic armies triumphed on the Continent in the 1620s, so Arminians came to seem papists, or at least semi-papists, in disguise: the fifth column that would prepare England for a return to Catholicism. The reluctance of Arminians to concur with the Puritan identification of the pope with Antichrist, and their readiness to countenance the coexistence of the English and Roman Churches, heightened Puritan suspicions.

Charles I was no Catholic, but there were momentous consequences to his marriage, in 1625, to the Catholic daughter of Henry IV of France, Henrietta Maria, who became the focus of papal and Catholic intrigue at the Stuart court. Charles grew devoted to her and was susceptible to her political advice. The bond between them encouraged suspicious interpretations of the king's own religious policies. Whereas his father had preserved a balance between the rival parties in the Church, he firmly backed the Arminians and rapidly promoted them. Their respect for ceremony and decorum appealed to that aesthetically sophisticated king, who saw in them a means to the inculcation of political obedience. In the evangelical impulse of Puritans, by contrast, he detected sedition in disguise. Arminian clerics duly obliged him, and provoked outrage in parliaments, by backing Charles's stance over taxation and the law. From early in his reign his political and religious programmes were, and were seen to be, of a piece.

After the dissolution of 1629, knowing that he could not finance wars without parliamentary support, he made peace with France and Spain. Over the next decade the supporters of his diplomacy relished England's exemption from the bloodshed of the Thirty Years War and lauded the prosperity which peace brought. Puritans, whose contacts with foreign Churches the king now curtailed, despaired at his desertion of Continental Protestantism, and applauded the lightning victories in Germany won on its behalf by Gustavus Adolphus, King of Sweden, who filled the European role that in Puritan eyes should have been Charles's.

The king's ecclesiastical policy was supervised by William Laud, Archbishop of Canterbury from 1633. An old man in a hurry, who for decades had longed to see the court and Church purged of their Calvinist components, he shared the king's view of parliaments and Puritans. MPs looked to Magna Carta as a sacred text of the liberties that were now under threat. Laud replied that the document 'had an obscure birth from usurpation and was fostered and shown to the world by rebellion'. No more than Charles was he a Catholic, though the papacy, which offered him a cardinal's hat, held hopes of his conversion. He knew that his programme was damaged by its association in the public mind with the growing influence, especially in the late 1630s, of Catholics at court, who were emboldened by the protection of the queen and by the holding of the Mass in her chapel and in London embassies where English Catholics were openly admitted.

Laud's vision of the Church was medieval and English. He aimed to restore to it, and to its clergy, the political role and social standing of which the Reformation had deprived them. He secured the appointment of his friend the Bishop of London, William Juxon, as Lord Treasurer, and of clergymen as JPs. He battled to recover Church lands and wealth, often at the expense of the laity. He saw hypocrisy in opponents of his churchmanship among gentry whose families had profited from the dissolution of the monasteries, and who in the churches had built grand pews, or erected flamboyant monuments to themselves and their ancestors, while leaving the fabric of the buildings in disrepair and the clergy underpaid.

Among the laity, even non-Puritans were alarmed by Laud's clericalism and were puzzled by the king's support for it. The crown's powers had been increased at the Reformation in order that it could keep churchmen, who had given medieval kings so much trouble, in their place. Might Laud's readiness to ally so closely with Charles, it was asked, be explained not as the fruit of loyalty but as a means to restore to the Church a power which, in the future, could be turned against less sympathetic rulers? Laud's brisk use of the church courts, especially the Court of High Commission, to bring Puritan or otherwise recalcitrant clergy and laity to heel aroused fear and indignation. He also deployed the Court of Star Chamber, which in 1637 sentenced three Puritan pamphleteers who had defied his censorship of the press, William Prynne, Henry Burton and John Bastwick, to imprisonment and physical mutilation. Three years later, on the downfall of Laud and of the regime he served, their return to freedom was hailed by a huge throng. For his authoritarianism, like anti-popery, gave Puritanism a width of appeal which its teachings could not have won by themselves.

Laud's agents transformed church interiors by removing communion tables, round which the celebrants had customarily gathered in the body of the building, to the east end, where they were railed off as altars and where the administering priest acquired a sacerdotal role. 'The altar', declared Laud, 'is the greatest place of God's residence upon earth.' Puritans who opened a fund for the better provision of preaching found their initiative suppressed by him. Another affront to Puritans was the reissue in 1633 of the Book of Sports, which with royal encouragement promoted the practice of communal pastimes on Sundays. The book, first published in 1618, had been less contentious under James I than it was in the polarized world of Charles I, where a number of clergy were deprived of their livings for refusing to read its text from the pulpit.

For whereas a laissez-faire approach to diversity of worship in the parishes had largely prevailed under James, it now yielded to the attempted enforcement of conformity. In the face of that pressure, Puritans faced troubling dilemmas. Should they assert their beliefs, or should they conceal them? Should the clergy among them accommodate themselves to idolatrous practices, and so retain their posts and their influence over their congregations, or repudiate those practices and face eviction and prosecution? The autocratic face of the Laudian Church was at its most aggressive in the dioceses of Matthew Wren, who, as Bishop first of Norwich

and then of Ely, presided over much of the Puritan heartland
of East Anglia. It was largely from East Anglia that Puritans
left to serve the Gospel overseas. Some exiles went to
Protestant Holland. Thousands went to New England, that
'howling wildness' as they biblically called it, to build the
colony of Massachusetts, though a great many other Puritans
who had contemplated emigration eventually stayed behind,
among them some of the political leaders who would confront Charles I in 1640.

Charles and Laud destroyed the base which the Church
of England had established in national sentiment. Laymen
and clergymen who under James had thought of themselves
as its loyal servants were now viewed from Whitehall and
Lambeth as its enemies. Yet until the mid-1630s, even
perhaps until some point in 1639, the king's policies in
Church and state seemed unassailable. Ingenious methods,
compatible with the letter of forgotten laws, were found for
raising revenue. Men whose wealth had, it transpired, obliged
them to present themselves for knighthood on his accession
were fined, as were others who were discovered to have
broken regulations governing the royal forests.

Those expedients, however, could only be used once.
Of profounder import was the levy of ship money, which
in 1637 created, through the defiance of the Buckinghamshire gentleman John Hampden, who provoked a test
case by refusing to pay it, what one observer called 'the
greatest cause according to the general opinion of the world
ever heard out of parliament in England'. The tax, collected
on a new system of allocation which provoked irritation
both by its novelty and by its effectiveness, financed
Charles's shipbuilding programme. Since ships protected
the nation, it was hard to argue against the government's

decision to extend the tax from the coastal counties, where it had been levied on previous occasions, to the whole country.

The issue was the one that had been raised by the 'loan' a decade earlier: the crown's claim to hold emergency powers of taxation and to be judge of the emergency. This time there was no emergency in sight. What made the dismay widespread was the judges' verdict, by seven votes to five, in the crown's favour. It was widely and rightly believed that the judiciary had yielded to royal pressure. If judges would not protect the subject's liberties, who would? The lawyer, historian and MP John Selden, no Puritan but a vigilant guardian against both royal and clerical encroachment on the legal system, remarked that the king's coronation oath 'is not security for our property, for he swears to govern according to law; now the judges ... interpret the law, and what judges can be made to do we know'.

Yet Charles's 'new counsels', for all the resentment they caused, succeeded in the short term. For all we can tell they might have prevailed in the long term if his problems had been confined to England. The crown balanced its books, and in the short term the resistance to ship money was worn down. But whereas the constitutional crisis of 1626–9, which had launched the 'new counsels', had been an English crisis, that of 1640–2 was a British one. The collapse of his authority in 1640 followed from events in Scotland, and the move to civil war in 1641–2 from ones in Ireland.

It was in Scotland that Charles committed political suicide. As in England, his deeds of provocation brought political and religious grievances together. The Stuarts had been glad to get out of Scotland, which they visited as rarely as possible. Ill-informed about Scottish (as about Irish) law and politics, the absentee Charles left his councillors at Edinburgh caught between uncomprehending autocratic decrees from Whitehall and the fury of the two great forces of Scottish society, the nobility and the Presbyterian Church, the Kirk. The nobility he provoked by muddled legal and administrative reforms that seemed to threaten their prominence in government, and by claiming, with dubious legality, the right to revoke the grants of the royal and monastic lands that had come into their hands since the Reformation.

Admittedly it was not easy to rule contiguous kingdoms with divergent institutions and traditions, for diplomatic and domestic policies pursued in one country had ramifications for the next and were scrutinized in it. Charles's contemporary Philip IV of Spain brought disaster on himself by his attempt to standardize the obligations of subjects to the crown in his Iberian kingdoms. James I had wanted to be king of a united Great Britain, but was thwarted by anti-Scottish sentiment in his southern kingdom. His absentee rule of Scotland had its successes, among them the patient and tactful introduction of an element of episcopacy, an institution which he admired in England, alongside the Scottish Presbyterian system. Here as elsewhere, Charles exchanged tact for confrontation. In 1637 he imposed a new Prayer Book on the Scots, which bore provocative resemblances to, as well as some provocatively anti-Calvinist distortions of, the English one. Scottish worship, which turned on preaching and extemporary prayer, and on the simple and communal commemoration of Christ in the sacrament, was to yield to alien set forms and to a sacerdotal eucharist. New powers given to the bishops threatened the Presbyterian structure of the Church.

The riot in St Giles Church in Edinburgh upon the first use of the Prayer Book in 1637 swelled into the national protest movement that in the following year produced the National Covenant, whose signatories affirmed their commitment to Scotland's own forms of worship. That potent document proclaimed their allegiance to the king, but indicated that their loyalty depended on his observance of Scottish laws. The Scots had a stronger tradition than England not only of Presbyterianism but of radical political theory. They were readier to call kings to account, though it took Charles's own provocations to push them, by 1639, into a willingness to go to war. Charles, having raised an army to enter Scotland to enforce obedience, found that the Scots had raised a stronger one.

Though the two sides drew back, and reached a truce at Berwick in June, the episode had destabilized his rule in England, where the raising of his forces had aroused intense opposition and a widespread refusal of taxation. Why should English subjects fight and pay for a war to enforce on Scotland a religious and political programme akin to one already so divisive in England? Charles's ill-disciplined army wrought destruction on the counties through which it passed, and suffered large desertions. Against that disordered background his leading critics in the two kingdoms risked the charge of treason by making secret contact. At last, in April 1640, the financial drain of the Scottish crisis reduced Charles to the expedient he had avoided for eleven years, the calling of an English parliament, the 'Short Parliament' as posterity knows it. Yet his attitude to the institution had not changed. He expected the parliament simply to vote supplies to meet his military needs. The Commons responded with a tart intimation that until 'the liberties of the House and kingdom be cleared, they knew not whether they had anything to give or no'. After three weeks Charles dissolved the assembly.

It was a critical moment, for at that stage many MPs would have responded readily to conciliatory measures. When, in November, he had to call another parliament, the mood of opposition had hardened. On dissolving the Short Parliament the king breached convention, and incensed the laity, by allowing the clergy's parallel institution, Convocation, to continue sitting. It passed orders, 'canons', which intensified both the content and the authoritarianism of the Laudian programme. Yet Laud himself was no longer the king's most feared adviser. That was now his ally the Yorkshireman Thomas Wentworth, newly created Earl of Strafford, who had run Charles's government in Ireland from 1633. He returned to England in 1639 and became the driving force behind royal policy.

In Ireland, Strafford had adopted brisk methods to heighten the crown's power and break its critics. Now he urged Charles to do the same in England and Scotland. Like Charles and Laud he equated Puritanism with sedition. He declared that, since the Short Parliament had evaded its financial responsibilities to the king, Charles was 'loosed and absolved from all rules of government'. But Strafford's plans for the reconstruction of royal authority were destroyed in August, when the Scots sent their army into England. It routed the English at Newburn outside Newcastle, and occupied the city.

The king's authority was in tatters, and the impossibility

of ruling England without the consent of the leaders of the shires was exposed. Twelve prominent peers petitioned him to summon another parliament, and a council of peers which he summoned at York in September was of a similar mind. Charles gave in. The new parliament which met on 3 November, the 'Long Parliament', would sit for thirteen years. By the time it assembled, Charles had reached an agreement with the Scots that involved the humiliating abandonment of his ecclesiastical policy there. It also obliged him to meet the high costs incurred by the occupying Scottish army in the north of England, which was to remain until the treaty was signed. Only the English parliament could supply the money. He was at his subjects' mercy.

The Long Parliament had two initial strengths: its unity, and the skill, cunning and resolution of its leadership. During its first year scarcely a voice defended Charles's deeds in Church or state. In normal times the management of parliament was organized by the royal ministers. Now the collapse of Charles's authority left a vacuum of leadership, which was swiftly occupied by able and powerful critics of royal policy: in the Lords the Earls of Bedford and Warwick, in the Commons John Pym, 'King Pym' as his enemies called him, though he had effective allies, among them two figures whose opposition to ship money had brought them national recognition, Hampden and his counsel Oliver St John.

Parliamentary leadership was not easy, especially in the Commons, much the larger chamber, whose 500 or so members valued their independence and their right to be

heard on matters great and small. The traditional procedures
of the House were geared to the assistance or debate of
initiatives by the government or by private members, not to
the formation of policies independent of the crown. With
time an increasing proportion of the Long Parliament's
business was entrusted to standing or ad hoc committees,
whose membership and methods the leaders, as dis-
agreements opened among them, vied to control. Yet debates
in the Commons, with their unpredictable shifts of mood
and sympathy, still had to be won.

Then there were the difficulties of coordinating the two
Houses. In the assault on Charles's misgovernment the Lords
were less bold than the Commons, whose more adventurous
spirits, now as until the abolition of the upper chamber in
1649, chafed at its inhibited response to the national crisis.
Only in collusion with the leaders in the Commons could
the more radical peers make progress in the upper House.
In religion, too, the Lords were less militant than the
Commons. Warwick, an outsize and jovial personality, had
in recent years sponsored piratical and colonizing ventures
in the New World, a project which had attracted a number
of the crown's other critics too, and which may have given
him and them a front for conspiracy. The aim of harrying
the Spanish overseas empire brought Puritan aims and
connections together with commercial ones. Warwick also
commanded, through his control of church livings and
through the influence of his friends and relations, a powerful
Puritan network in Essex. Yet the earl himself was not
conspicuously Puritan. Neither was the more courtly and
politically more moderate Bedford.

By contrast the fear of popery and Arminianism, and of
the takeover of the government by them, was the underlying

impulse of Pym's every political deed. A financial official without a significant landed estate, he owed his seat in parliament to the patronage of his ally Bedford. The two men did not want to starve the government of funds, unless as a temporary tactic. They knew that the institution of parliament would survive only if it made it worth the crown's financial while to summon it. They wanted to pressure Charles, through their parliamentary backing and with the promise of revenue, into putting them and their friends in charge of the government, which they would then reform. The king did reluctantly give high posts to some of the parliamentary leaders, but he then avoided their counsel. Hopes of more effectual appointments ended in May 1641 with the death of Bedford himself, who was to have been made Lord Treasurer. In negotiating with Charles the leaders had to watch their backs, for behind parliament stood the constituencies, which strengthened and heartened parliament with petitions endorsing its attacks on Charles's mis-government, but which were endemically mistrustful of money-raising initiatives from whatever quarter.

The leaders' unstated alliance with the Scots, too, was a liability as well as an advantage. The Scottish army in northern England enabled Warwick, Bedford, Pym and their allies to hold the king to ransom, but they were suspected of cynically protracting the treaty for that purpose. Despite, and some-times because of, its affinities with English Puritans, that army was highly unpopular, especially where it was quartered. The upkeep of the English forces to keep watch on it was an additional burden. Only in August 1641, nine months after the parliament had met, was the agreement reached that enabled the Scots to return home the following month and the English forces to disband.

Yet so long as it concentrated its fire on the king's misrule, the parliamentary leadership carried almost all before it. Charles, politically isolated, surrendered to a startling series of legislative initiatives, whose passage seemed to their supporters a miraculous deliverance from the oppression of the previous decade and a half. Chief among them were the abolition of Star Chamber and High Commission, the outlawing of ship money, a Triennial Bill (a provision that no more than three years should lapse without a parliament), and a bill forbidding the dissolution of the present parliament without its own consent. The king's leading ministers were impeached or else fled abroad. Laud was placed in the Tower, where he would remain for four years before being attainted and beheaded.

The urgent target was Strafford. Here the leaders ran into difficulty, for the charge of treason against him, which rested on an allegation that he had advised Charles to use an Irish army against his English opponents, would not stick. After Strafford had run rings round his prosecutors the impeachment of him was abandoned, and parliament instead passed a bill of attainder against him, a procedure that required the Houses merely to declare, rather than prove, that the earl had had treasonous designs. After agonized deliberation the king signed the bill. He would never forgive himself for that concession, which he convinced himself had been a dereliction of kingship and thus an offence before the God to whom alone his exercise of his royal office was accountable. Strafford's execution on Tower Hill in May was witnessed by an enormous and exultant audience.

The legislative and political triumphs of the parliament were mostly achieved by that month. Yet Charles had sacrificed the goodwill which his concessions might have earned. In the hope of saving the earl's life he gave countenance to a plot, organized by courtiers close to the queen, to overawe parliament by seizing the Tower of London and by bringing south the army that was facing the Scots. The revelation of the conspiracy frightened and angered the backbenchers. In June Pym, playing on that mood, demanded two sharp reductions of the royal prerogative. Parliament must have the power to veto crown appointments to high office; and the county militias, the nearest thing the country had to standing forces, must be put 'in a posture of defence' under lieutenants chosen not by the crown but by parliament. To those conditions Charles would never have agreed. In August, to parliament's further concern, he went to Scotland in the hope of building a following there. During his visit a scheme was devised within his court to seize the leaders of the Scottish opposition, perhaps even to assassinate them. What then might he attempt against the English leaders?

In October a graver alarm raised the crisis to a new pitch. It came from Ireland. About three-quarters of the Irish population were Gaelic Catholics, who had experienced two waves of colonization, one in the distant past, the other recent. First had come the Norman settlers, the 'Old English', who remained predominantly Catholic but had acquired a Protestant component. Then there were the post-Reformation settlers, the Protestant 'New English', who had taken political control in the sixteenth century, and whose power and numbers increased greatly under the early Stuarts. With the crown's encouragement, lands that had been confiscated after the defeat of the protracted

Gaelic insurgency of the last years of Elizabeth were shared out in a plantation scheme.

Ireland, like Scotland, was a back door to England. A Spanish force had landed there in 1601. The plantation was designed both as an impediment to foreign threats and as a means of 'civilizing' the Irish, in English eyes a savage and barbarous race. Though many of the new settlers lived in Ulster, they were outnumbered there by Presbyterian Scots, who retained close ties of kinship and political sympathy with their co-religionists in their homeland, as the English settlers did with the opponents of Charles I's policies in England. Across the narrow sea from Ulster to Scotland there stretched not only Presbyterianism but an opposing Gaelic and Catholic network, to which the Ulster settlement was intended as a counterweight. For in Scotland as in England the Reformation had been incomplete.

Strafford's rule in Ireland, which had strengthened the crown's power and enhanced its revenue, was in an inadvertent sense even-handed, for it alienated every section both of Anglo-Irish and of native society. It also provoked trepidation in England. The goal of his ally Laud in the Church had its counterpart in Strafford's plans for the state, for both men strove to overcome interest groups which seemed to them to put their privileges and private concerns before the common good. Strafford's devices for raising the royal revenue, and his support for Arminianism within the Protestant Irish Church, looked part of a trend to autocracy throughout Britain.

Yet it was Strafford's fall, not his rule, that brought tumult to Ireland. The crisis of royal authority now spread there from England and Scotland, but with a difference. In the other two countries the breakdown derived from

the crown's assault on the entrenched forms of Protestantism. In Ireland it arose from a Catholic rebellion.
The anti-Catholicism that swayed in Westminster, Edinburgh and Ulster heightened the long-held fear of Irish
Catholics that their religion would be driven from their
land. Catholic leaders, aristocrats who were essentially
loyal to the crown but hoped to increase their own influence on it, took advantage of the weakening of the
government's authority in Dublin to stage a pre-emptive
rising.

They lost control of their followers. A wave of popular
protest spread through and beyond Ulster and took a course
that proved catastrophic for Ireland's future. Religious and
economic distress (especially among families dispossessed
by the settlements of recent decades), and the violent tactics
with which the executive in Dublin responded to the rising,
incited the massacre perhaps of around 2,000 Protestants,
perhaps of a great many more. It seems that in Ulster
around one in five of the Protestant population was killed.
In some instances men, women and children were herded
together to be tortured or drowned or burned. The horror
provoked by the butchery, which lay beyond English com-
prehension, was real enough, but soon the numbers of the
slain and the sufferings of the victims, dead and alive, were
being massively and luridly exaggerated in accounts brought
by refugees and sedulously spread in print.

The rising created a new and more dangerous atmosphere
at Westminster. It intensified still further the fear and
hatred of popery, which had thrived on the instability of
1641. It brought parliamentary demands for the disarming
of Catholics in England, where, in the panic induced by
the Irish rising, they were groundlessly accused of arming

and gathering in large numbers. The same mood brought the impeachment of the queen's confessor. It also raised the issue that eventually made war in England inescapable, the control of the armed forces. For if the rebellion were to be suppressed, who would be entrusted with its suppression? The insurgents told themselves and others that the rising had been endorsed by the king, their fellow victim of Puritan and Covenanter bigotry. That slur on him may have been believed by Pym, who in any case could not afford to allow Charles to send to Ireland an army that might then be used against parliament or its Scottish allies.

In 1642 king and parliament did agree to the appointment of the Earl of Leicester, a man of torn loyalties in the English conflict, to be Strafford's successor as lord lieutenant, but he never visited the kingdom. All he managed was the dispatch of a few hundred men under two of his sons. In the year ahead the two sides in the English civil war, needing every soldier for themselves, gave attention to Ireland only when its fate affected their own military prospects. As a result the country escaped English control until 1649. In its place it suffered a devastating civil war, during which the contending parties divided and regrouped in an array of allegiances so complex and mutable that no narrator has succeeded in making them more than momentarily intelligible.

By the time of the king's return from Scotland to Whitehall in late November 1641, the conflict within England had found a new focus: the City of London and its teeming population, which had increased six-fold over the previous century. It now accounted for nearly a tenth of the country's numbers, which had themselves doubled over the same period to reach around five million. Nowhere were the nation's disputes contested more fiercely than in London's streets and churches, or among its trading companies, its rulers of wards and parishes, its gatherings and gangs of apprentices. All the power groups of the civil wars would have an eye on the hard-fought politics of London, and all the changes of regime over the 1640s and 1650s were facilitated or followed by coups within the City government which brought the new rulers' allies there to power.

In the annual elections to that government in December a wave of Puritan sympathy, and of antagonism to London's commercial oligarchs, gave allies of Pym the command not only of Guildhall politics but of the City's trained bands. Parliament looked to them for protection against the swaggering officers from the recently disbanded army of the north who were ominously assembling, with other intemperate company, round the king. Charles laid a charge of treason against Pym, Hampden, and three other members of the Commons, together with the peer Viscount Mandeville. On 4 January 1642 he led about eighty armed men into the Commons and demanded the arrest of the five members.

Just in time they had slipped away by water into the City. The king was defiantly answered by the Speaker, and the anger at Charles's action played into Pym's hands. When the king rode into the City to call for the members to be handed over, London's governors and crowds cried out to him, 'Privileges of parliament!' The Commons temporarily withdrew from the Palace at Westminster to sit under the City's protection at the Guildhall. Less than a week after his attempted coup, Charles, having lost control of the capital, abjectly departed from it. When he returned in 1649 it was after defeat in civil war and as a prisoner facing execution.

WAR

With the king's departure from London, civil war seemed likely if not unavoidable. But both sides wanted the other to start it and so to bear the responsibility for it. Until the summer they fought with paper, appealing to the nation with indignant ripostes to each other's declarations and messages and protests. Parliament, which in the previous year had been brazenly assuming a series of executive powers, now stepped up its demands of the king, in effect requiring that he hand over the choice both of the personnel and of the policies of the government. Legislation passed by parliament in February 1642 awarded it command of the armed forces. Since the king would not sign it, parliament called the measure an ordinance – the 'militia ordinance' – rather than an act, but the two Houses claimed binding authority for it, as they would for the succession of ordinances passed at Westminster during the remainder of Charles's life.

Yet his opponents feared the taint of rebellion. The crown and the Houses of Parliament were customarily seen as complementary or interacting bodies. No one was used to thinking of them as rivals for power. Now constitutional theory scrambled to keep up with the transformation of the legislature into a body that was in effect aspiring to sovereign authority. Parliament adopted a number of argumentative tactics. It revived the medieval doctrine of the king's 'two bodies', which distinguished between his 'office', on which the law and constitution turned, and his 'person', which, when it perverted or deserted the exercise of the office, must yield its powers to parliament, which had to do his job for him. It maintained that the nation had 'entrusted' its representative body to deal with a king who himself had broken the 'trust' that he had accepted in his coronation oath. It asserted its own status as the high court of the land and thus the ultimate arbiter of constitutional contest. And it claimed the very emergency powers which the king had invoked in collecting the forced loan and ship money.

In raising their demands, the parliamentary leaders apparently calculated that the king, who had left London with a tiny following, would be unable to enlarge it. Yet their assertiveness provoked a reaction within their own ranks. The unity that had enabled Pym to steer through reforms until the summer of 1641 had dissolved. In November 1641 the Grand Remonstrance passed the Commons, after an impassioned debate, by only eleven votes, with MPs drawing swords in the chamber. Despite its claim to represent the nation, this parliament like its predecessors tried to keep its deliberations to itself, free from the pressures of public opinion. Pym changed that rule. The Remonstrance, ostensibly an address to the king, was an appeal over the heads of the more cautious parliamentarians to public opinion. There were more alarming extra-parliamentary methods too. The proceedings against Strafford had been aided by the arrival of crowds at Westminster which, with the connivance of Pym and his friends in the City, harassed and threatened members of the two Houses who opposed that initiative. The tactic became familiar. Riots and popular disturbances were common enough in seventeenth-century England, but the breakdown of the constitution in 1641–2 gave them new targets and perhaps a new frequency and ferocity.

Fear for public order was one of the factors to work to the king's advantage. From early in 1642, deviating into political sense, he helped his cause by skilful if insincere concessions. The hardliners who had come to dominate his counsels in 1641 were joined by more moderate figures, who had supported the reforms achieved by parliament in that year but who believed them to have gone far enough. Among the recruits was Edward Hyde, the future Earl of Clarendon, whose great narrative of the civil wars, *The History of the Rebellion*, would do as much as any book to shape the Tory tradition, but who, with many supporters of the king in 1642, had been dismayed by his policies in the 1630s. Other moderates persuaded Charles to issue a cleverly worded redefinition of his powers, which implicitly renounced his non-parliamentary methods. His publicists now defined the constitution as a mixture of three estates, king, Lords and Commons, which held in balance the three classical principles of government, monarchy, aristocracy and democracy.

With the reaction in politics came one in religion. It surfaced among men resistant to the bolder forms of Puritanism. Many of the parliament's initiatives in religion, for the encouragement of preaching and preachers, for the eviction of ungodly or 'popish' ministers from their livings, or for the affirmation of Calvinist doctrine, commanded wide support. At least, few dared speak against them. Other religious issues, however, caused deep division. In politics, MPs attacked the policies of Charles I but not the constitution which he was judged to have abused. By contrast the hostility aroused by Laud extended beyond his policies to the very institution of episcopacy which had implemented them, and through which, even if Laud himself were defeated, his goals might be pursued again. In the second month of the Long Parliament a mass petition from London demanded an end to episcopacy 'root and branch'.

The issue split parliament between abolitionists and those who would have been content with reforms to curtail the powers and the secular activities of the bishops. Many MPs agreed at least this far with the crown, that episcopacy was an aid to the principles of order and hierarchy. 'If we make a parity in the Church', warned one member, 'we must come to make a parity in the commonwealth'. A bill for abolition was introduced in May 1641, but proved too divisive to pursue. Instead the leadership concentrated on the punishment of individual bishops and on a bill, which Charles despairingly signed in February 1642, for the removal of the episcopate from the House of Lords, where he had generally been able to count on its votes.

Yet the supporters of both measures had used crowds to frighten the bishops themselves from attending parliament. Puritanism, whose mainstream adherents prided themselves on their sobriety and lawfulness of conduct, had acquired some violent agencies and allies. The smashing of stained-glass windows, and other acts of iconoclasm, by soldiers or mobs had been common since 1639. In September 1641 the Commons, vainly hoping to bring order to what was becoming a recklessly anti-authoritarian process, issued an order, without the Lords' agreement, for the demolition of altar rails and the destruction of images and crucifixes. When parliament then adjourned for a month, MPs discovered the hostility that the measure had provoked in the localities.

Puritanism had problems enough within its own ranks. It thought of itself as the guardian of orthodox doctrine and worship against the sinful innovations of the Laudian Church. Yet its reforms in religion and politics excited wild hopes and beliefs among its followers, which orthodox Puritans could not restrain. The sense of convulsion and expectation was heightened by the collapse of the crown's and Church's powers of censorship, and by the consequent proliferation of pamphlets aimed at a wide readership. A wave of doctrinal speculation and innovation spread through the London parishes and into the provinces.

In that new mood, Puritans who adhered to familiar teachings and forms of worship were themselves accused of putting human tradition before the word and experience of God, and so of being tainted by the spirit of popery against which they had ostensibly been contending. The gravity of Puritanism, too, was spurned by exclamatory populist preachers, who defied the rule restricting the pulpit to ordained clergy, as many others would do during the civil wars. Lay preachers espoused doctrines, and commanded an appeal to wide audiences, that seemed to challenge not only orthodox religion but social cohesion. That, asserted Anglicans, was where the Puritan insistence on the autonomy of the individual conscience must lead. The vocal role acquired by women in sectarian debate compounded the sense that the natural order was being subverted. The unleashing of new religious forces, which would tear the

Puritan cause apart, was one of the many unforeseen consequences of the parliamentary initiatives of 1640–2.

In religion as in politics, Charles's advisers persuaded him to make timely concessions. He appointed non-Laudian bishops to vacant sees; portrayed his ideal of the Church as a middle way between Laudian and Puritan excesses; and promised to restore 'the established and true reformed Protestant religion as it stood in its beauty in the happy days of Queen Elizabeth, without any connivance of popery'. In the initial stages of the Long Parliament, when grievances in Church and state had joined, Puritanism had seemed to speak for the nation. The identification, hard as Pym struggled to preserve it, could not survive the disintegration of the parliament's unity. In 1642 Charles built a party, albeit one motivated more by reaction against parliament than by any enthusiasm for him. More than two-fifths of the Commons, and a higher proportion of the Lords, left Westminster in the king's cause.

The slide to civil war from January was slow. It involved a series of local skirmishes and of struggles for the control of garrisons and coastal towns and arms depots. Only in August, when the king raised his standard at Nottingham, was the fact of war formally recognized. Despite his recent victories of public opinion, his military following was slow to form. From January, leading his little band through the kingdom, he cut a pitiful figure. Supposedly the defender of the realm, he lost the means even to defend himself. Agents of parliament seized the ports and magazines of Hull, whose governor humiliated him by refusing him entry to the town, and Portsmouth. The navy deserted him and resolved to serve under parliament's nominee the Earl of Warwick. By July the raising of parliamentarian regiments was in full swing, whereas only a few hundred soldiers attended the raising of the royal standard the following month. When a parliamentarian army under the Earl of Essex, whose father had been executed for treason late in Elizabeth's reign, set out from London it held all the advantages.

Yet as summer turned to autumn the picture was transformed. The king moved to Shrewsbury, from where he was able to mobilize what became the heartland of his support: Wales, the Welsh marches, and the west Midlands and the north of England. He was aided by reports of the conduct of parliamentarian soldiers who had allegedly smashed organs, ripped clerical garments, urinated in fonts. In late September a division of the parliamentarian army rashly attacked a royalist force under the king's nephew, Prince Rupert, son of the Elector Palatine, at Powick Bridge, close to Shrewsbury. The parliamentarians were routed.

The first major battle followed in mid-October. After Powick Bridge the king, with an army now almost equal in size to Essex's, had headed towards London. At Edgehill in Warwickshire he found himself confronted by the earl's forces. It was in that intense but indecisive encounter that both sides met the shock of war. The opposing armies, raw and ill-trained, suffered heavy casualties. Next day, after a cold night in the fields, they backed off. The threat to London persisted until November, when only the gathering of forces from within and around the capital, who faced the royal army at Turnham Green near Brentford, dissuaded the king from an assault. He retired to Oxford, which would be his own wartime capital.

Both sides had begun the war with the supposition that a single battle might decide it. Instead, as the scale of campaigning was reduced for the winter, they began to sense the magnitude of the attrition ahead. Few had wanted the war. It was one thing to feel strongly about the rule of Charles I or about the parliamentary response to it, another to think it right to fight over them. Throughout the wars the term 'unnatural' would be used of them, to allude to the self-division of a nation which honoured its harmony, and to the bloodshed and enmities that split families and friends and neighbours. When contemporaries asked themselves how the war had come about, their first explanation was the sinfulness of the land and its provocation of God's wrath. The long, rarely broken peace of the early Stuart era, and the prosperity it had produced, were held to have bred heedless wantonness.

If the war seemed an affront to the regular order of things, so did the making of choices between crown and parliament. There was, as one of the regional declarations that resisted the descent into war put it, a 'new and unnatural logic' when parliament was 'severed from the king the head thereof'. 'A good understanding between king and parliament', declared another, was what 'every good man did desire more than his own life'. During the war parliamentarians would tell themselves that they were fighting 'for king and parliament'. In 1642 demands spread through the counties for an 'accommodation' or 'middle way' that would preserve the crown's rights and restore the subject's liberties. In some counties local rulers formed pacts of neutrality or, with the aim of protecting their communities from intrusion by either side, built fortifications or even tried to raise their own forces. It was a doomed hope. The two sides in the civil war were able to raise and sustain large armies, against which county boundaries were no defence. Except to the east of a more or less vertical line from the Lincolnshire Wash to the south coast, almost every part of England saw fighting, as did much of Wales. Outside parliamentarian London and East Anglia, and stretches of royalist territory in the far north-west, there were few areas where either side established or maintained unchallenged control. Most towns and counties were divided.

Nonetheless regional patterns of allegiance did emerge. In the main, parliament was strongest where Puritanism was strongest. The king had most support where the intellectual content of recent debates about politics and religion had made least impact; or where Catholics could be levied in large numbers; or where there were magnates, the Earls of Newcastle and Derby, who could still command something like a feudal following – though it is a mistake to think of the royalist cause as essentially aristocratic or hierarchical, for quite as much as parliament it had a self-generated popular following.

If the king rallied much of the north and west, parliament's strength lay in London and East Anglia and the Home Counties. Yet the geographical distribution of sympathies conceals almost as much as it reveals. The regions did not spontaneously declare for the sides on which they predominantly fought. They were commandeered for them. Parliament seized territory which the king, in travelling north in 1642, had abandoned, whereas Charles controlled areas to which he brought his army. To promote the king's cause, say, in Norfolk, once risings on his behalf had been crushed in 1643 and the county been secured for parliament, or in London, where there was much resentful royalism, would be to invite the plunder or confiscation of one's estate or goods and the levying of punitive taxation. Defiance on parliament's behalf in the areas firmest for the king would have been comparably self-destructive. It was easier to swim with the tide, or else to keep one's head down. The latter course became ever harder to sustain, especially for the more substantial landowners.

If the geography of allegiances was far from straightforward, so was its sociology. The intensity of modern research on the war dates from a controversy of the 1940s and 1950s, fought with polemical power by R. H. Tawney and Hugh Trevor-Roper and Lawrence Stone and Christopher Hill, which explained the war, largely or wholly, as a conflict of classes: between aristocracy and gentry, or between rich gentry and poor gentry, or between a rising bourgeoisie and a declining feudal order. The hypotheses of those scholars have surrendered to the research which they stimulated. There were indeed sociological differences, as there will be in any political conflict, but while they sometimes help to explain men's responses to the crisis of 1642 they do not account for the crisis itself, which has no discernible place in any long-term development of the social structure.

In any case the differences are far from clear-cut. The majority of peers supported the king, but the minority on parliament's side included leading generals and politicians. The older and the more substantial gentry families, and the urban oligarchies, were marginally likelier to be found on the king's side than on parliament's. In some regions a difference has been detected between the more tightly knit of the rural settlements, to be found in areas of arable farming where both social deference and communal organization and sentiment prevailed, and less cohesive ones, in areas of pasture and woodland. The first are thought to have inclined to royalism, the second to parliamentarianism, though both the geographical extent and the explanation of the contrast are debated. As a rule, merchants dreaded war and its economic consequences. Towns feared annexation as strategic bases and as garrisons, a fate that indeed awaited a high proportion of them. Yet there was some keen urban partisanship too. The mill and clothing towns, especially in Essex and Somerset and Lancashire and Yorkshire, were almost wholly parliamentarian, because they were so largely Puritan, as were other towns which rallied round parliament. Equally, cathedral cities produced more royalists than most other towns.

For the nearest thing to a clear division between the two sides is a religious one; and though religion, then as always, took on the sociological colourings of its adherents, the appeal of both Puritanism and Anglicanism extended across a wide social range. While by no means everyone on either side was devout, or was exercised by the religious issues, the king's firm supporters were in general committed to the practices enjoined by the Prayer Book, while the majority of parliament's wanted reform at the Book's expense. However, there is a distinction to be drawn. While for many people religion supplied the principal motive or impulse to take arms, far fewer took their justification from it. During the widespread inspection of consciences that was prompted by the rival calls to fight in 1642, even zealous Anglicans or Puritans paused to wonder whether the constitution, and the laws of the land, permitted a resort to warfare in God's cause.

The paper war of 1642, in which the two sides sought to disprove the other's legitimacy, brought such questions to the fore. Yet much of the nation may have been swayed less by propaganda, or by reasoned argument, than by instinct or traits of character or by the example or pressures of other men. Individuals are likely to have been persuaded or antagonized by the stands of landlords or neighbours or clergymen. Long-standing local connections and rivalries mingled with or even overrode issues of principle. Thus the divided affiliation of Leicestershire, when the county was reluctantly drawn into the war, turned on the conflict between the two leading families of the shire, the Greys, who backed parliament, and the Hastings, who, though like the Greys having a Puritan following, became royalist.

Allegiances, fierce in many cases, were in others fickle or calculating or conditional. During the war a smattering of peers and gentry and army officers went over to the enemy, though their conversions won them small respect on the side to which they changed. Some families seem to have ensured that they were represented on both sides, so that the victors among them might enjoy their spoils and shield their defeated relations from reprisals. People who longed for the war to end alleged that there were men who cynically strove to prolong it: foreign mercenaries in the armies; native soldiers raised among the poor and unemployed; contractors for military supplies. On both sides there were hardliners with reasons of principle for fighting the war to the finish and for opposing the intermittent peace negotiations and the compromises they might bring.

Yet the parliamentarian and the royalist causes were broad coalitions. Moderates on the two sides could have more in common with each other than with the zealots with whom they found themselves allied. They were nervous of winning an outright victory, which on the parliamentarian side would hand power to the political and religious radicalism that throve on the war effort, and on the royalist one would allow Charles to revert to his pre-war policies with an army now behind him. When, in 1644, the royalist MPs gathered as a parliament at Oxford, the king found them almost as troublesome, and as hostile to extreme policies, as his earlier parliaments, and paid as little attention as possible to what he called a 'mongrel parliament'.

Nonetheless, contrasts of outlook between royalists and parliamentarians can be identified. They can be traced not only to differences present at the outset of war but to the binding experiences of the fighting, of its din and smoke and terror and excitement; to the forging of ties which extended from regiments to civilians who organized or argued over the war effort; and to the formation of collective self-images, which can give distinctive identities to embattled causes and sustain their morale. Admittedly the two sides caricatured each other. When, in the crisis of the mid-winter of 1641–2 that immediately preceded Charles's attempt on the five members, the pejorative terms Cavalier and Roundhead were deployed on the London streets, they began a process of distortion that has endured to this day. Neither before nor during the war was there a marked difference of physical appearance between the members of the two sides. There were merry parliamentarians and earnest royalists.

Yet whereas parliamentarians spurned the term Roundhead, royalists were ready to be called Cavaliers. In its initial, hostile, usage the term alluded to the cruelty of Spanish troopers, *caballeros*, in the Netherlands, but it was annexed by royalists to conceptions of honour, courtly loyalty, and social order. 'A complete Cavalier', a royalist preacher told soldiers at Oxford, 'is a child of honour. He is the only reserve of English gentility and ancient valour, and has chosen to bury himself in the tomb of honour' rather 'than to see the nobility of this nation vassalized'. Honour paradoxically obliged the courtier Sir Edmund Verney of Buckinghamshire to fight for Charles against Verney's own principles. Verney declared that his 'conscience' required him 'in honour and gratitude to follow' a master whom he had served, and whose 'bread' he had 'eaten', for nearly thirty years. So he risked his life, and lost it at Edgehill, for 'things' – especially 'the bishops, for whom this quarrel consists' – which the same 'conscience' could not 'defend'. Many others likewise chose sides with ambivalent feelings.

Parliamentarians spoke of honour too, but it did not occupy the heart of their cause or produce as many displays of bravery as it inspired in royalists. Parliamentarian courage took its strength from religion. The cause of the Church in turn animated royalists, among whom, alongside colourfully hedonist adherents to the cause, we find men of sober spiritual devotion, as alert as parliamentarians to the workings of divine providence in the war. Cavalier soldiers, no less than Roundhead ones, were obliged to attend services and sermons, and were liable to punishment for irreverence. Even so, the royalist struggle to preserve the ecclesiastical order did not incite the degree of belligerence that was fired by the Puritan determination to overhaul it.

The recruitment of parliamentarian soldiers who saw themselves as God's instruments, and fought ardently in his name, is commonly and rightly associated with Oliver Cromwell, whose 'Ironsides' were initially recruited among

Puritans in his native Fenland, but it was also favoured by other parliamentarian commanders, some of whom, long beleaguered with their forces in royalist areas, sustained themselves and their armies from one hardship to the next by prayer and Psalm-singing. Inside and outside its armies the parliamentarian cause throve on the detection of parallels between the history of the Israelites, the chosen nation of the Old Testament, and England, which Puritans saw as the chosen one of the new dispensation, where idolatry would be cast down and the Reformation completed. Sermons to parliament, to local governors, to Puritan congregations and to soldiers reminded their hearers that the successes of their cause owed nothing to their worthless selves, everything to the inexplicable grace of God.

Parliamentarian defeats brought the abasement and self-inspection of the Puritan soul. Victories brought it exaltation of spirit. As the royalists fled from the field at Langport in Somerset in 1645, the courageous Thomas Harrison, then a junior officer but later a leading political and military figure, was heard 'with a loud voice' to 'break forth into the praises of God with fluent expressions, as if he had been in a rapture'. In the same year he took part in the capture of Basing House, the Hampshire stronghold whose largely Catholic occupants were ruthlessly treated by the parliamentarians under Cromwell's command. 'Cursed be he that doth the Lord's work negligently,' proclaimed Harrison as he shot a soldier who in civilian life had been a comedian in Drury Lane.

Harrison was a butcher's son and a lawyer's clerk. Many who shared his convictions rose with him from low social origins to high command, not because promotions were made with any design of social redistribution but because, amid the tentativeness of many parliamentarian commanders, such men were so effective in battle. 'I had rather have a plain russet-coated captain that knows what he fights for and loves what he knows', declared Cromwell, 'than that which you call a gentleman and is nothing else.' During the grim and protracted siege of Taunton, which tied down royalist forces in the autumn of 1644, the town's parliamentarian governor, Robert Blake, later the victorious admiral of Cromwell's navy, told his besiegers that 'the honour and reputation of a gentleman' mattered little beside 'the goodness and power of an Almighty Saviour', in whose cause he would always trust and never surrender.

The English civil wars have no place in the evolution of military strategy. There were many Englishmen (though more Scotsmen and Irishmen) who had volunteered for service in the Thirty Years War and had acquired skill and experience in them. Of the leading generals, the king himself, Newcastle, Cromwell and the Earl of Manchester (formerly Lord Mandeville, the peer whom Charles had tried to arrest in 1642) were among the few who had not served in that conflict, though in a number of regiments it was left to a subordinate officer, who had known service abroad, to provide the expertise lacking in his higher-born colonel. The Anglo-Scottish conflict had also brought some military experience, of a painful kind. Dutch and Swedish methods of warfare were widely studied and were imported into the English struggle. Military engineers were recruited from abroad.

Yet if a decisive military achievement emerged from the war, it lay not in new skills in the disposition of troops or equipment but in the imposition of discipline. The contrast between the achievement of Cromwell, in restraining his cavalry after their successful charges and in bringing them back into the fray, and the failure of Prince Rupert, the king's leading general, to prevent his horsemen from chasing his opponents from the battlefield in search of plunder, had decisive consequences. In the handful of big battles, fought in open country, the two sides followed European convention in drawing up their cavalry on either side of the infantry, which consisted of pikemen, laden with their long weapons, and musketeers. Yet most of the war was fought in different conditions: in sieges; or in skirmishes in streets or churchyards or in or around villages.

On both sides a number of armies were raised, some national, some local, though there was a tendency towards amalgamation as the war persisted, for separate forces struggled to liaise effectively or to respond to shifts of military fortune in other zones. There was no single or clear shape to the war. If either side had a single objective, it was the return of Charles to the capital, the difference being that royalists wanted his prerogatives to be at least partly restored by victory, whereas parliamentarians looked to see them at least partly curtailed by defeat.

The early advantage lay with the king. In the months after Turnham Green it was the more nervous parliamentarians who called for peace and compromise, Charles who disdained them. In the summer of 1643 the war went his way. He had three principal armies: his own in Oxford, which took on the Earl of Essex in the Thames Valley and Buckinghamshire, and thwarted the earl's designs on the royal capital; Newcastle's in the north, which after hard-fought engagements in Yorkshire marched into Lincolnshire and threatened East Anglia; and that of Sir Ralph Hopton, a critic of Charles's pre-war rule who had rallied to him in 1642, and whose forces now marched east from their base in Cornwall and routed the parliamentarians at Roundway Down in Wiltshire. The great port of Bristol fell to the king. In the south-west and the west only Gloucester, on whose fate the control of the Severn Valley and its supply lines depended, held out for parliament.

In his desperation in 1643 Pym turned to the party with which he had collaborated before the war, the Scottish Presbyterians. They agreed to enter the conflict in return for a parliamentarian commitment to introduce compulsory Presbyterianism in England and Ireland. Only thus, they reasoned, would their own ascendancy in Scotland be secured against external intervention. Parliament bound itself to the treaty by the Solemn League and Covenant, a pledge of support for the Scots' war aims that was to be imposed on the population of England – or anyway on the parts of it under parliamentarian control – for subscription. Not for the only time in the civil wars, a requirement to declare a partisan loyalty caused agonies of conscience, not least because of the apparent contradiction with earlier vows, in this case the oaths of allegiance and supremacy which the crown had received before the civil wars.

Nonetheless the Covenant secured the arrival of the Scottish force of about 20,000 men, significantly larger than any single army in England. It crossed the border under the Earl of Leven in January 1644. The Scots played a large part in the war effort of that year, but distrust between the allies gradually reduced their effectiveness. So did the emergence in Scotland of a royalist army under the Earl of Montrose, which obliged Leven to look over his shoulder and made his army reluctant to march too far south. The Scots were present at the great battle of Marston Moor in Yorkshire in 1644, but not at the major encounter of the following year, Naseby, fought further south, in Leicestershire.

The decision to involve the Scots in an English conflict divided parliament and gave royalist propaganda a useful weapon. Unfortunately for the king's own image, he too had resorted to outside aid in 1643, to less military advantage and at a greater cost in public sentiment. His hopes of securing an army from fellow monarchs on the Continent never materialized, but while Pym was securing the Scottish alliance Charles sanctioned a truce in Ireland, the 'Cessation', in order to free around 10,000 Protestant soldiers to fight in England.

The Cessation was interpreted in England as the appeasement of Irish Catholicism. After the collapse of English authority, Catholic Ireland had created its own provisional government, the Confederate Association. Like the main civil-war groupings in all three kingdoms, it was a coalition of diverse views and interests. At one end stood the larger landowners, whose main objectives were a reconciliation with the king and the defeat of his English enemies. At the other, appealing beyond that elite, was a more radical party, led by bishops and clergy and by returning exiles. In exchange for peace with Charles it wanted the restoration of the Catholic Church in Ireland and the recovery of land from the Protestant settlers.

For Charles to seek the pacification of the Confederacy was risky enough. Later in the war, when his cause wilted, he went further, seeking the backing of the pope and the Confederacy's armed support. Parliament captured and published letters which revealed the extent of his intrigues and of the concessions he was ready to make. The public identification of royalism with Catholicism was heightened by developments in Scotland, where Montrose's army consisted largely of Irish Catholics with clannish ties to Scottish co-religionists. Montrose's supporters were often less interested in succouring the king than in pursuing ancient quarrels with the Campbells, whose leader, the Marquis of Argyll, was a dominant force in the Covenanter movement. Montrose provided the king with a series of brilliant victories in 1644–5, but his cause collapsed around the time that the English royalists were suffering fatal reverses.

We have been looking ahead. Even before the arrival of the Scottish army in England at the start of 1644, the king's fortunes were declining. Whereas, in the summer and autumn of 1642, the tide had turned in the king's favour, the same period of 1643 brought an opposite development. The Earl of Essex, in the one bright period of his generalship, relieved Gloucester and defied a royalist assault in a major battle at Newbury in Berkshire. The Earl of Newcastle's position in Yorkshire and Lincolnshire weakened. Over the course of 1643 two new and large parliamentarian armies were formed, one under the MP Sir William Waller, the other the army of a confederation of the East Anglian counties, the Eastern Association, the only one of a number of attempts made by both sides to create regional associations and armies that achieved much success. Led by Manchester with Cromwell as his second-in-command, the Eastern Association's forces confronted the royalist threat from the north.

During the first half of 1644, despite occasional royalist

successes, the waning of the king's cause continued. Its defeats in the south-west, the north-west, and in Lincolnshire and Yorkshire enabled parliament to concentrate on the north of England, where the Scottish regiments joined with Manchester's and with local forces to besiege York. They were thwarted by Rupert, whose swift march across the Pennines enabled him to relieve the city and confront the parliamentarians on Marston Moor, a few miles to its west, on 2 July. Perhaps around 45,000 soldiers took part in the largest battle of the war, indeed maybe the largest gathering of men that had ever met on English soil. Though the royalists were routed, the outcome was long uncertain. Leading parliamentarians were driven from the field before Cromwell's cavalry turned the course of the battle, which lasted into the moonlit night. Dawn found thousands of soldiers groaning on the field of battle, and bodies strewn for miles on the road to York, which the parliamentarians soon took. The royalists' ascendancy in the north had been permanently lost.

Yet in the ensuing months they staged a remarkable recovery in the south, thanks largely to divisions and strategic errors on the parliamentarian side. The king's main forces, vulnerable to Essex's and Manchester's armies, were spared fatal attack by the conduct of the two earls. Essex perplexed parliament and his military colleagues by marching away from the heart of the war into Cornwall, where he was humiliatingly defeated in a series of engagements at Lost-withiel. Manchester, who had brought his exhausted army from York into Lincolnshire, was loath to move it again. When he did eventually join forces with Waller in the autumn, the generals bungled two chances to defeat the king in the area around Newbury.

The high recriminations which followed led parliament to a radical reorganization of its forces. By a 'self-denying ordinance', all peers and members of the Commons were stripped of their commands, though Cromwell, a chief instigator of the measure, contrived to secure exemption from it. Regiments of existing armies were purged and reconfigured, and were placed under the command of Sir Thomas Fairfax, who had fought heroically in his native Yorkshire and elsewhere in the north, but who as yet had little national standing. Cromwell was made Fairfax's second-in-command of what was now the main parliamentarian army, the 'new model' as it quickly became known. It made an uncertain start, but its formation was vindicated when it brought the king and Rupert to battle at Naseby on 14 June, where perhaps around 30,000 men fought. As at Marston Moor the outcome was long in doubt, and as at Marston Moor the role of Cromwell's cavalry in the victory was critical. Again there was heavy slaughter, and again the bodies were strewn across miles of countryside.

Naseby was the making of the new model: of its self-esteem and of the bonds between officers and soldier. Soon after the battle the army embarked on its arduous and conclusive advance through the south-west. After taking Bristol from Rupert, who paid the price of dismissal by the king, it carried all before it in Devon and Cornwall. Rupert's generalship had brought dash and confidence to the royalist cause. Now he had lost heart. His enemies at court tried to convict him of treason for surrendering the port, and although the charge failed he went abroad, his role in the war finished. Through England and Wales the royalist forces were by now heavily depleted. The new model finally took Oxford in May 1646, though not before the king had slipped out of his capital and made his way to Lincolnshire, where he gave himself up to the Scots. He ordered his remaining garrisons to surrender on such terms as they could get, though a handful of them clung on, the last of them, Harlech in Wales, yielding the struggle only in March 1647.

Why did parliament win the war? It had advantages which, though barely evident in the earlier stages of the conflict, became conspicuous with time. Controlling London and East Anglia, the more populous and prosperous area of the kingdom, it had superior resources of manpower and wealth. In few of the larger battles did the king's forces match parliament's in numbers. The Roundheads out-numbered the Cavaliers by three to two – perhaps more – at the first of the two decisive encounters of the war, at Marston Moor, and maybe by as much as two to one at the second, Naseby.

Even so, recruitment was an enduring problem for par-liament as well as for the king. Both sides initially depended on volunteers, some ardent for their cause, some glad of the money or the adventure, and on the raising of local forces, in parliament's case by the authority of the militia ordinance, in the king's by the medieval device of com-missions of array. Yet from 1643 the arbitrary and some-times brutal conscription of infantry was commonplace. When one area had been bled dry of recruits, the process moved to the next. Mutiny, desertion, and transfers of allegiance to victors or captors were common. The turnover among the population of the soldiery was high.

Cavalry, in which in the earlier stages of the war the

royalists had the advantage in both quality and leadership, presented both sides with fewer problems of discipline and loyalty. Men who could ride horses were on the whole of higher social stock than the foot soldiers, who were paid at about the average wage of agricultural labourers. The cavalry were better remunerated and could ride in search of food or shelter. Yet perhaps the two most striking feats of collective valour in the war were deeds of infantry: the first at Marston Moor, where soldiers under the Earl of Newcastle's command, who had been disorderly during the recent siege of York, fought to the death with their ranks unbroken; the second in the new model army's capture of Bristol, where foot soldiers scaled the city walls immediately beneath enemy fire. On the same army's formation only months earlier, the infantry had been a rabble.

The king had the greater problems of supply. Oxford was far from his main sources of munitions, which lay largely in the iron-producing regions of south Wales and the Forest of Dean, and of men. Much of the fighting took place on or near his supply lines. Control of the corridors between his armies, in the counties to Oxford's west and north and north-east, was heavily contested. Whereas Charles's supporters in parliament's heartland had to preserve low profiles or at best give him limited and secret aid, his own areas of strength contained enclaves of determined parliamentarian resistance, among them Pembrokeshire and the northern clothing towns.

On parliament's side the command of London brought administrative, economic and military advantages. Charles had to do without the departments of Whitehall, which were taken over and ably adapted by MPs. Parliament exploited the industrial capacity of the capital and its suburbs in the production of arms and military clothing. It raised large and, at least in the earlier stages of the war, predominantly eager forces of Londoners. The capital's established printing presses facilitated the rapid production of propaganda. The command of the City's wealth was of critical significance. For although land remained the prime measure of wealth and social status in the mid-seventeenth century, there were vast resources of mercantile wealth and expertise to tap. Enterprising merchants lent money to parliament, or negotiated contracts for the supply of arms and provisions, or administered the collection of customs and other taxes.

Parliament's control of the navy was an obvious benefit, but not an unlimited one in a war fought mainly on land. In coastal engagements, combined operations between land and sea were only occasionally effective. The king in any case was able to commandeer ships for his cause in the west country, where he controlled ports and long stretches of coastline. The parliamentarian navy did not prevent him from importing foreign arms and men. But it did impose permanent restraints on him. In 1643 the troops which were brought from Ireland in his cause, and which might otherwise have formed a single force, had to be divided for fear of naval interception and were dispersed across regions and regiments.

Yet the parliamentarians' victory was far from inevitable. Much hung on the judgements and errors and fortunes of the leaders. What, it has often been asked, if the king had marched on London when the capital lay open to him immediately after Edgehill? What if Rupert had declined battle at Marston Moor, or not antagonized his ally the Earl of Newcastle, who commanded the city of York, in the prelude to the fight? Or if Sir George Goring, the able but bibulous general in the west, had obeyed the king's orders and brought his forces to join the king's before Naseby, or if Rupert had succeeded in dissuading Charles from giving battle there? There is no unambiguous answer to those questions. The crucial military judgements were often finely balanced, and alternative choices would have created alternative dilemmas.

Parliament had its own disadvantages, whose severity is concealed only by the eventual outcome. It saw itself as fighting for law against lawlessness. Yet while its success in 1642 in formulating legal and constitutional claims in justification of its challenge to the king indicates the limits to the awe that monarchy inspired, those arguments had an element of strain. Disobedience to the monarch went against political instinct. The charges of treason and rebellion which the two sides aimed at each other came more easily to the lips of Cavaliers than of Roundheads. In raising money for the war, Charles was of course resorting, as through the 1630s, to non-parliamentary taxation. Yet non-royal taxation, and the non-royal legislation that imposed parliament's will on the nation, were more profound departures from conventional thinking. Fear and mistrust of Charles did give a sense of legitimacy to the war against him so long as its purpose seemed defensive. But parliament had no agreed programme for victory, and had difficulty in vindicating it.

The methods of that conquest were still harder to justify. For under the pressures of war, parliament resorted, in pursuit of constitutional ends, to ever more unconstitutional means. The host of committees which it set up in the capital and the counties bluntly overrode law and custom in seizing estates and money. MPs who had indignantly declared ship money to be illegal used methods, and raised income on a scale, that put that earlier initiative in the shade. Parliament's want of scruple was vindicated by one of its leading politicians, Lord Wharton, on the ground that the king's opponents were 'not tied to a law, for these were times of necessity and imminent danger'. Just so had Strafford urged the king to set legal restraints aside in 1640.

The fiscal and administrative methods of royalists are more difficult to chart, for after their defeat they prudently destroyed most of their wartime records, just as defeated Puritans would impair the future study of the regimes of the 1650s by burning papers at the Restoration. It does seem, however, that the king, perhaps having learned a lesson from the pre-war decade, was more respectful than parliament of the traditional forms and agencies through which the consent of local communities could be won. Yet as royalist fortunes declined, those proprieties yielded to the urgent need for cash and troops, and to the ruthless raising of them.

It is hard to say which side was the more divided. At Oxford, Rupert, young, impetuous, scornful of politics in general and of English politicians in particular, joined other 'swordsmen' in contempt for Charles's civilian and legally minded advisers such as Hyde. Courtiers were split over the desirability of Catholic and foreign aid, the course favoured by the queen. Fearful of impeachment by parliament, she had gone abroad in 1642 to win foreign supplies and support. She returned to court in 1643, but slipped abroad again in the following year. In her absences her cajoling letters urged her divisive policy on her husband. Royalists split, too, over the wisdom and propriety of constitutional or religious concessions that might produce a negotiated peace. There were ruinous incompatibilities of personality, especially between the suave and astute Lord Digby, who became Charles's leading adviser towards the end of the war, and Rupert. It was hard for Charles even to keep his own household in order.

Yet at least he had the authority, as no one in parliament could have, to impose his political and military decisions. At Westminster conflicts were fought out not at a court with an arbiter at its head but in rival cabals, headless committees, tempestuous debates. Although the departure of the royalist MPs from Westminster had strengthened Pym's hold, fresh divisions undid that gain. His death from cancer in 1643, and Hampden's demise in battle the same year, accentuated the problem of authority. If Pym had a successor it was the inscrutable Oliver St John, the former lawyer of Hampden. For all his gifts of political manipulation he lacked Pym's or Hampden's stature. Soon he was embroiled in the partisan strife which Pym had striven to transcend. They turned not only on politics but on religion, a subject of more profound quarrel among parliamentarians than among royalists.

Until the end of 1644, too, relations between military and civilian were even more troubled on parliament's side than the king's. Essex, much concerned with his own standing and image, baulked at his subordination to parliament. He fumed at the creation of the army of the popular general Waller, in which he saw a rival to his own, and at the diversion of resources to it. He opposed the treaty with the Scots. What he wanted was not a decisive victory over the king, which many looked to the Scots to help achieve, but a settlement honourable to both sides. Manchester had the same aim. The displacement of the two earls from the high command in 1645 had its parallel on the king's side, where the amateurish and aristocratic generals of the early stages of the war, and commanders wary of offending the localities in which they raised or quartered their troops, were pushed aside by swordsmen with brisk professional methods. Yet there was no overhaul of the royalist armies on a scale to match the creation of the new model.

It was the new model that won the war, as it would win the second civil war in 1648 and the epic campaigns in Ireland and Scotland in 1649–51. Its triumphs witnessed to its discipline and to the courage inspired by it. Yet the achievement was civilian as well as military. It would have been impossible without administrative changes which, again, the royalists were unable to rival. Here as elsewhere the civil wars showed how much managerial ability had gone unused in the ordinary course of monarchical politics. The records of the assessors and scribes and account keepers who served the standing parliamentary committees, both in the centre and in the localities, reveal an impressive degree of literacy, numeracy and administrative competence.

At a higher political level the skills and instincts acquired by the MPs and merchants and financiers who ran the war effort, and who devised and managed the techniques that paid for it, had lasting impacts – as both Cromwell and Charles II might ruefully have reflected when their parliaments insisted on inspecting public accounts. In 1645 the new model's advocates secured control of the committees which communicated with the army, and efficiently centralized the provision of pay and supplies. They also conceded to Fairfax a degree of independence in the making of military decisions that his predecessors, who had chafed at under-informed orders from Westminster, must have envied.

Fairfax brought to parliamentarian generalship the readiness to take risks that Rupert had given the royalists. Civilians, and sometimes soldiers too, had fretted at the cautious strategic thinking of the earlier parliamentarian generals, Essex, Waller and Manchester. On both sides there were grumbles when battle was evaded, or when towns were besieged – a generally long and often unsuccessful process – rather than stormed, or when men or supplies were diverted from the field armies to garrisons distant from the action.

Caution nonetheless had its logic, especially in the earlier stages of the war, when both sides knew so little of the other's strengths or positions or movements, and when the planting of garrisons was essential to the securing of territory and its resources. Even when we allow for the exaggerations of complaining generals, shortages of equipment and manpower were a recurrent restraint on initiative. Charles might have won the war in 1643 if he had had the gunpowder to press his advantage at Newbury. The soldiery was repeatedly depleted by sickness or hunger or desertion. Debilitating too was the exhaustion visited on infantry regiments by their interminable marches in pursuit of an elusive enemy or of provisions.

Bad roads compounded the problem, as did erratic military intelligence and in some cases primitive or unreliable maps. It was a cumbersome war. Carriages, weighed down by artillery or other supplies, or transporting great bulks of money for soldiers' pay, moved slowly with large escorts or sank in the seas of mud brought by the dreadful weather of the decade. The wet setting in which Charles raised his standard at Nottingham, only for it to fall down overnight in the wind, foreshadowed the seemingly incessant rain of the campaigning seasons of 1643 and 1644, and the still worse summer of the second civil war in 1648. In the autumn of 1644 parliamentarian forces which might have broken the king in the area south of Oxford were brought to a standstill by disease and bad weather. Winter campaigns brought their own hazards, among them the melting snow which reached the armpits of the Scottish army as it waded through Northumberland in January 1644, and the bitter frost that awaited the new model on its strenuous advance into the west two years later.

Contemporaries feared that the war would bring 'a German devastation': a repeat of the havoc wrought by the Thirty Years War in the Habsburg lands. They thought particularly of the sack of Magdeburg in 1631, which laid the city waste. Nothing quite like that happened, but countless towns and villages and farms were badly damaged. Sometimes the ruins were repaired only decades later, if at all. Victors, their pay usually in arrears, were accustomed to the rewards of plunder, to which the release of tension after battle gave an edge of elation.

Some commanders, seeking the sympathy of the population, urged restraint on their troops. Fairfax imposed it. Others, however, preferred terror and brutality, especially Rupert, whose notorious raids were visited on Lancastrian towns in 1644 and whose soldiers hideously sacked Leicester shortly before the battle of Naseby. As the war progressed, vicious reprisals became more frequent. Troops recruited from outside England provoked special antagonism, particularly those from Ireland. In July 1644 a group of Irish prisoners, exempted from quarter by Essex on the ground of their nationality, were executed in cold blood. The royalists retaliated by lynching a dozen parliamentarian prisoners. After Naseby more than a hundred women who had followed the royalist army, and who were thought, perhaps wrongly, to be Irish, were slaughtered by the victors.

Yet within England atrocities were at least confined to a numerically small scale. They were newsworthy because they were exceptions. Codes of conduct governing the granting of quarter on surrender, and the treatment of the enemy's wounded or the burial of its dead, were generally observed. Admittedly the conventions afforded only limited protection. Some prisoners taken in the conflict endured harsh conditions; dead or prostrate bodies were commonly stripped of clothes or weapons after battle; and, although some provision was made for the care of the wounded and the relief of the maimed, the land would long be haunted by beggars incapacitated by the fighting. Yet there were mollifying influences. The battles were fought for control of the nation, not, as civil wars sometimes are, between the centre and movements for independence. The awareness of common nationhood was a restraining bond. Ties of kinship and friendship that crossed the party lines held savagery back. So did grief, which was voiced not only for the loss of neighbours or loved ones but for the fate of the divided land. In the aftermath of battles the sight of the fallen, whether friends or foes, would wrench the heart.

It was a hard war to idealize. Abraham Cowley's royalist poem of 1643, *The Civil War*, which attempted to elevate the war into epic literature by bedecking it with Cupids and Furies and angels, scarcely worked. So, except when used for mockery, did resort to the uplifting language of medieval and Renaissance chivalry. The high achievements of imaginative literature or of political reflection to emerge from the civil wars – the verse of John Milton and Andrew Marvell, the prose of Clarendon and Thomas Hobbes and James Harrington – were responses to defeat and disappointment or to the nation's social and political breakdown. Only men with an uncomplicated sense of allegiance to God or king could reflect without discomfort, at the time or afterwards, on their own parts in a conflict which intensified the discord it was meant to resolve.

Some commanders, it is true, allowed themselves, well after their return to civilian life, to be known by their military titles. Yet in the few, and mostly colourless, military memoirs produced by the war, designed to vindicate their authors, there is some troubled writing. Neither courage nor heroism quite hid the guilt, or anyway the unease, of civil war. The visual record of the conflict, if we except printed matter and woodcuts, is minimal. Even royalism, the more aesthetically aware of the two sides, produced nothing to parallel in aspiration, let alone achievement, a work such as Velázquez's celebratory triumph of the Spaniards over the Dutch at Breda in 1625.

If we could imagine the same conflict being fought a little later in the century, perhaps in the 1660s, amid the growing biographical awareness of the age of Samuel Pepys, we might expect to find accounts of the war that took us further into the feelings of the participants. The same decade, the era also of the start of the Royal Society and of emerging statistical enquiry, might have left us a stronger base of evidence for reckoning the sizes of armies and the numbers of casualties. From the imperfect sources that we do have, it has been reasonably estimated that more than one in ten of the adult male population bore arms. Military enlistment angered localities by reducing the supply of labour, which is one reason why recruiting officers, especially at harvest time, looked for servants or the unemployed to fill the ranks of infantry.

The death rate was very high. Many more died in skirmishes or small battles than in large ones, though deaths in arms seem themselves to have been outnumbered by casualties of the diseases, especially typhus and dysentery, which spread through and beyond the armies. If the figures which have been reckoned by informed modern guesswork are even roughly reliable, a larger proportion of the population died as a result of the civil wars than of the Great War of 1914–18, though the numbers for the simultaneous conflict in Scotland were apparently higher and those for Ireland much more so.

The war, which created industrial production on a huge scale, produced its economic beneficiaries too. There were the manufacturers of guns and pikes and swords and gunpowder and saddles and wagons and all the ancillary components of military equipment. There were the suppliers of cloth coats – the main distinguishing marks, when there were any, of military uniform – and of shoes (generally cheap and short-lived) and stockings. Yet to most of the civilian population the war brought only deprivation. The areas most affected were ones close to the fighting or to the towns and country houses that were converted into garrisons. In general towns suffered still more fighting and destruction than the countryside. Suburbs were ripped up to clear space for attacks on towns or for their defence.

Across the land, it seems, around 11,000 houses may have been destroyed and their occupants made homeless. Fire, especially where there was thatch, was a persistent hazard. It was started sometimes accidentally, sometimes by fire-pikes or grenades thrown to destroy property or to swamp the enemy in smoke.

War and its preparations brought disruption wherever they touched. The capitals of the two sides, Oxford, a university city turned into political and military headquarters, and London, were massively fortified. The centres and routes of England's trade, its ports and rivers and vales and passes, were blockaded by the armies which vied for their military uses. Londoners shivered without their coal from Newcastle. But at least the capital escaped the fighting. Heavy as the burden of the war was, its distribution was uneven. An arc drawn from Somerset through Oxford up into Nottingham-shire would pass through the regions that in general had most to bear.

Soldiers needed to be fed and sheltered. Though the basic military diet, of biscuits and cheese, could be brought from afar, livestock had to be requisitioned in vast quantities. Horses, which themselves had often been requisitioned, devoured meadows and great quantities of oats. Bedding and kitchen equipment were forcibly taken from households. Communities in the contested regions, where rival forces alternately advanced and retreated, suffered not only dis-proportionate destruction but a double jeopardy, for people who were constrained to assist one side would in turn be punished by the other. The occupants of houses on which soldiers were compulsorily quartered were supposed to be given tickets so that they could reclaim the cost after the war. The tickets were often supplied, but repayment by parliament was far from uniform and on the defeated king's side was impracticable.

The scale of the taxation which sustained the war effort was unrecognizably large. Taxes were collected by agents of the hated county committees, which were staffed by the social upstarts who alone would do that and other administrative work for the war effort, and who thus usurped the traditional rulers of the shires. Their intrusion was made harder to bear by the partial breakdown of the assizes and quarter sessions, to which communities looked for legal processes and for the resolution of local conflicts. Resistance to the committees was inhibited by the military presence. A massive monthly land tax, the 'assessment', was supplemented by a novel sales tax, imposed by both sides: the excise, a levy detested at the time and for generations to come. The seizure of the estates and rental incomes of enemies, and the operation of the administrative machinery that was developed to allow the victims to reclaim their lands on payment of substantial fines, scarred national and local feeling, even if confiscation was often ingeniously evaded.

By 1645 a protest movement had arisen against the war itself, especially in regions where fighting or military occupation had been most intensive. Spreading from the Welsh marches to the south and west of England and to south Wales, it produced something like a third force, which gathered armies of a size to alarm parliamentarians and royalists alike. These 'clubmen', named after the primitive weapons which some of them carried, demanded an end to hostilities and accommodation between king and parliament. They called for the return of law and peace and order and of the spirit and institutions of local government. Though the movement lacked staying power, it signalled the national mood of exhaustion and disillusion. Yet when peace did return in 1646 it solved nothing. It was a peace which the king, who had lost the war, believed that he could either turn or end to his own advantage.

3

REGICIDE

It was one thing for parliament to defeat Charles I, another for it to know what to do with him. The parliamentarians, unless with marginal exceptions, were not republicans. They had pledged themselves to restore the king. But they were not magnanimous in victory. Having borne the costs and strains of war, they were determined to deny him any scope for returning to his pre-war ways. Among the terms on which parliament and its Scottish allies insisted were parliamentary control of the armed forces for twenty years (at the end of which, if still alive, he would be in his later sixties), the abolition of episcopacy, the establishment of Presbyterianism in its place, the king's own subscription to the Solemn League and Covenant, and the punishment of a long list of royalists.

In response Charles sought to divide his enemies and resume his throne on favourable or even unconditional terms. He thought it his duty to God and to his kingly office to maintain his prerogatives and preserve episcopacy. Quarrels among the parliamentarians, who had come to hate each other almost or quite as much as they did him, gave him a strong hand, which he overplayed. He protracted negotiations with the various parties, offering shows of conciliation and making half-promises which were incompatible with pledges he was soon discovered to have made to other groups. The longer the war had lasted, the deeper the conflicts within parliament and among its followers had become. In politics the division was between a war party, which wanted to bring the king to his knees and impose a settlement on him, and a peace party, which wanted him restored by negotiation. With that issue there mingled a religious one which hit Puritanism at its heart: liberty of conscience. We must see how the two controversies came together.

Religious tolerance went against the grain of seventeenth-century thinking. In a society without a police force or, ordinarily, a standing army, the preservation of order will seem dependent on the coherence, even the uniformity, of ideas and beliefs. The coexistence of faiths within a nation's frontiers was generally assumed to be unattainable and undesirable. Few were convinced by the obvious exception, the limited and vulnerable toleration that had been granted to France's Protestants after its wars of religion.

Political and social anxieties mixed with theological ones, especially among Puritans, of whom the majority, while seeking liberty for their own faith, of whose truth they were certain, were determined to deny it to other doctrines, which they knew to be false. Archbishop Laud, the Puritans' enemy, had required external conformity to the rites of the Church. He was less worried about men's inner beliefs, save as they might prompt opposition to his programme. But orthodox Puritans, in whose thinking worship was to be reverenced not for its outward properties but as an expression of faith within, demanded the conformity of the soul itself. Not merely, they maintained, would heresy disfigure the community of believers. It would carry its adherents to hell, a fate from which it was the duty of Church and state, through compulsion if need be, to save them. In the common language of mainstream Puritanism, heresy was an infection, which only surgical or purgative methods would cure.

There was, however, an alternative position, which was rarely voiced before the 1640s but which won a powerful following during them. What the enforcers of orthodoxy saw as the guardianship of faith was in other quarters condemned as persecution. Salvation, it was argued, comes not through submission to a set of beliefs prescribed by human authority – the practice, after all, on which papists were accused of resting – but through the various and inevitably faltering process by which fallen men make their way, through their own understandings and spiritual exertions, towards God's grace. To interfere in that process, and to demand the correction of mistakes into which the believer might temporarily have strayed, was to risk cutting the lifeline of salvation. How, in any case, could true doctrine be known and defined? Might not the end of the Laudian Church, and the upheaval which followed it, betoken an extension of the Reformation, in which God's followers, newly freed from the blinkers of superstition that had survived it, would discover truths that even the great theologians of the sixteenth century had missed?

That hope is offered by John Milton, who in 1641 envisaged 'the reforming of Reformation itself', and whose plea for freedom of religious expression three years later, *Areopagitica*, described his fellow Londoners 'sitting by their studious lamps, musing, searching, revolving new notions and ideas', 'reading, trying all things, assenting to the force of reason and convincement'. There were limits to Milton's advocacy of liberty, which he would not have extended to blasphemers or atheists or Catholics or idolaters. Like most champions of the same cause he was concerned, not to establish what later generations would think of as the human right of free belief and worship, but to promote the Gospel against its adversaries. It was in that cause that he welcomed the proliferation of unorthodox beliefs which occurred with startling rapidity in the 1640s.

Some of them had existed in previous decades, mostly living underground, out of authority's sight. Others were born of the breakdown of political and ecclesiastical authority from 1640. In some cases the beliefs took apocalyptic forms: in others they derived from a rational scepticism which broke inherited certainties. Largely emerging from within Puritanism, they frequently assailed the most precious of Puritan convictions, the doctrine of predestination. They also challenged beliefs, which Puritans no less than other Protestants had taken over from Catholicism, about the Holy Trinity, about the fate of the soul after death, and about infant Baptism. For on those matters the Scriptures, which Protestant theology claimed as its foundation, gave doubtful support to it. The sect with the strongest pre-war history was the Baptists (who maintained that baptism should be an adult choice). Of the deviant religious groups of the 1640s they were the most conspicuous and influential, not least in the new model army. Though some of them, the 'Particular Baptists', were predestinarians, the more contentious of them, the 'General Baptists', rejected the Calvinist scheme as confidently as the Arminians had done.

In the expectant mood of 1641 that followed the nation's emancipation from the Laudian programme, orthodox

Puritans had hoped to make of England a new Jerusalem, uniform in belief. Instead they saw it become a hydra of sects and heresies, as certain as the nation's defects of morality to provoke divine retaliation. With doctrinal diversity came ecclesiastical fragmentation. Established members of congregations broke away from them and moved to or among other groups, or formed new ones. Puritans customarily looked forward to a close working relationship between magistrates of their own persuasion and godly clergy. They expected the state to enforce the doctrines which theologians defined. Now sectaries told them that Church and state should be divided, and God's spirit be liberated from the human institutions that restrained or perverted it.

Religious experiment throve on the printing press, which the civil wars brought into its own. Cheaply printed pamphlets, which before 1640 had been only an intermittent form of publication, were now daily occurrences. Copies of a majority of them were kept by the bookseller George Thomason, whose collection, now in the British Library, is a voluminous documentary source – though, since both it and the other great source for the period, the administrative records of central and local government, reveal more about the parliamentarian than about the royalist cause, research on the period has found more scope among the victors than the losers of the civil war. Attempts by parliament, and later by the republic and Cromwell, to reimpose the censorship of the press were only partially successful. This was the first age of journalism, when writers cultivated a brisk, plain prose that reached large audiences. Both sides in the civil war were ambivalent about the new medium. Nervous of the social forces, and of the power of public opinion, that it might unleash, they also competed to exploit it.

Here was another large unintended consequence of the wars: the restless expansion of political knowledge and opinion, a trend to which the recruitment of signatures for petitions or protestations also contributed. Weekly news-books, often controlled by the royalist or parliamentarian leaders or by factions among them, gave slanted reports of the war and its attendant controversies. One of the ablest of the editors, Marchamont Nedham, observed afterwards that 'in our late wars ... the pen militant hath had as sharp encounters as the sword, and borne away as many trophies'.

Important as political propaganda was, a higher proportion of publication addressed religious issues. Much of it concerned the government of the Church. Since the departure of the royalists from Westminster in 1642, episcopacy had been a less controversial issue there. The institution had ceased to operate in the areas controlled by parliament, which in 1646 abolished it. Political considerations had overcome the doubters: fear of the uses which a restored king might make of bishops; parliament's obligation to the Scots, who had made abolition a condition of their alliance; and the opportunity, irresistible to a parliament desperate to meet the debts incurred by the war effort, to sell the bishops' lands. But how would episcopacy be replaced? A synod of Puritan divines, the Westminster Assembly, met at parliament's behest in 1643 to devise an alternative machinery of ecclesiastical government. The majority favoured a Presbyterian system with a hierarchy of ruling bodies, ascending from the individual parish to small regions, from small regions to large ones, and thence to a national assembly, whose decrees would pass back down.

From that scheme a small but vocal body of divines dissented. They were committed to the system, which had grown up in New England, of Congregationalism or Independency, in which each congregation is a voluntary and autonomous association of believers. The dispute, which turned on interpretations of the evidence in the New Testament about the character of the primitive Church, would be fought hard throughout the wars. Yet it need not have been insoluble. Whatever the differences among the theologians, the power to decide lay with parliament, few of whose members were rigidly committed to either position. Most would have accepted a compromise, provided it met two tests: that it preserve the national unity of the Church, and that it protect the parishes, and the influence commanded by the leaders of local society there, from central interference.

What inflamed the issue was its connection to the principle of liberty of conscience. Intolerance was almost a cardinal premise of Presbyterianism. Congregationalism was intolerant in New England, where the state enforced it, and initially there seemed no reason why it should be tolerant in England. The Independent leaders in England were not 'separatists', the term that was used to describe people who broke away from the national Church. They did not challenge the parish system, which their voluntary gatherings were designed to supplement, not to replace. Gradually, however, liberty of conscience became a principle of the Independents, even if they were divided about its proper extent. Being in a small minority in the Assembly, they were obliged to look for allies outside it, where they found support among groups of laymen who dreaded religious compulsion. In parliament two tendencies came together against the intolerance of Presbyterian clergymen. Some MPs were persuaded by the spiritual arguments for liberty of conscience. Others – 'Erastians' as they were known, after the sixteenth-century thinker Thomas Erastus – were concerned above all to subordinate the clergy to the laity and the Church to the state. Hostile to bigotry from whatever quarter, they took the political and intellectual health of a community to need some scope for variety of opinion.

Outside parliament the Presbyterians found fierce adversaries in the sectaries. The Independents accordingly turned to them, too, and especially to the man who had become their most powerful champion, Oliver Cromwell. Cromwell's own ecclesiastical allegiances were vague enough to allow him to draw a coalition of Independents and sectaries and separatists around him. In the army of the Eastern Association he angered his superior, Manchester, in 1644 by fixing the promotion of such men. In the new model, unorthodox teachings spread swiftly. The unity and the victories achieved by soldiers of varied religious allegiances were proof to Cromwell that godliness and divine favour could cut across denominations. Liberty of conscience was the abiding preoccupation of his career, from inner conviction and also because of the support which the principle won him from religious dissenters.

The issues of Church government and liberty of conscience merged with the political conflicts within parliament. The mixture was irreversible from the time of the explosive quarrels of the winter of 1644–5, which produced first Cromwell's efforts to overthrow his military superiors, then a retaliatory attempt by them to impeach him, and eventually the overhaul of the parliamentarian forces. For as a rule (and with many exceptions), those MPs who shared the new model's eagerness to crush the king made common cause with the Independents, while those who sought an honourable peace with him allied with the Presbyterians. For that reason, and to the confusion of posterity, the terms 'Independent' and 'Presbyterian' were applied, as loose labels, to political as well as religious parties.

On both fronts the parliamentary leaders of the Independents were Cromwell's cousin Oliver St John and friend Sir Henry Vane, who as a young man had settled in Massachusetts and become its governor, only to quarrel irrevocably with its leaders over the principle of liberty of conscience. The two men had influential support in the Lords from Viscount Saye and Sele, who had been prominent in the pre-war opposition to the king, from Lord Wharton, and from the Earl of Northumberland. The Presbyterian leaders were Denzil Holles and Sir Philip Stapleton. Both of them, unlike those Independent leaders, had fought with distinction in the civil war. Their principal ally in the Lords, until his death in 1646, was their friend the Earl of Essex. They resented his removal from the army and the creation of the new model.

Pressures of war can bring unexpected reversals of alliance. It was the war party that, through the mediation of Sir Henry Vane, had brought the Scots into the conflict in 1643. But the Scots, abhorring the notion of liberty of conscience, soon discovered that Vane, Cromwell and their friends were abettors of heresy. They accordingly transferred their allegiance to Holles and Stapleton, who, having initially resisted the involvement of the northern nation, now looked to it as a counterweight to the Independents. Once the war was ended, however, the Scottish army became an embarrassment to the Presbyterian leaders. Its military record had been disappointing; it was costly to maintain and was hated wherever it encamped; and its unpopularity aided the Independents. Early in 1647 parliament bought the Scots off. After handing over the king to parliament, which settled him at Holdenby House in Northamptonshire, the Scottish army marched home in discontent. One half of its initial mission, the defeat of Charles, had succeeded, but the other half, the export of Scottish Presbyterianism, had failed.

Yet if parliament had wearied of the Scots, the king, before and after the departure of their army, saw opportunities in their grievances. The deterioration of the Scots' relations with the English parliament had provoked a reaction in his favour at Edinburgh. While his refusal to swear to the Solemn League and Covenant, or to pledge himself to the establishment of Presbyterianism in England, offended the Scottish hardliners led by Argyll, a more moderate group, headed by the king's kinsman the Duke of Hamilton, saw Charles's restoration in England as the best means to restore stability to Scotland. Meanwhile another development improved the king's prospects in negotiation more dramatically – though in due course it would be the destruction of him. This was the emergence of the new model army in 1647 as an autonomous and resolute political force.

Once the war was ended, it was essential to reduce parliament's armed forces and the taxation that sustained them. The military presence, which had at least been intelligible to the population as an inevitable but temporary burden of war, was harder to stomach when the fighting had ended, the more so because the late 1640s brought bad harvests, high prices, economic depression and some acute food shortages. Until a settlement with the king had been reached, however, the soldiery could hardly be disbanded altogether. The largest problems arose not from the well-disciplined new model, which occupied a series of quarters not far from London, but from the mutinous supplementary forces stationed further away, whose pay was heavily in arrears and who frequently and forcibly extracted money and provisions and shelter from town and country.

The payment of the soldiers, and their return to civilian life, might have been achieved easily enough had not the process become entwined with the struggle at Westminster for control of the parliamentarian cause. Between the end of the war and the execution of the king in January 1649, the fortunes of the rival parties oscillated, but in the spring of 1647 Holles and Stapleton held the upper hand. Though some of the outlying forces, among whose officers the Presbyterians had much support, were disbanded, it was the new model that Holles and Stapleton were determined to destroy. They resolved to send a number of its regiments to begin the reconquest of Ireland, under commanders who could be trusted to bring that country under Presbyterian rather than Independent control, and to disband the rest. Yet the pay even of the soldiers of the new model, who for the sake of the war effort had received favoured treatment in that as other respects, was badly behind. To their demand for it they added another: indemnity from prosecution at common law for such wartime acts as the seizing of horses from civilians.

When a number of regiments petitioned parliament on those counts, Holles's hatred of the new model exploded. To him soldiers were the servants of parliament, who had been employed to do its bidding and who were obliged to follow its orders uncomplainingly. He was indifferent to the new model's *amour propre*, to its pride in its victories, and to the costs of life and limb that it had borne. He persuaded himself that the agitation of the soldiery derived from an insurrectionary movement in the lower orders, for whom he had a violent contempt. Late one evening in March 1647, when a number of Independent MPs had gone home, he rushed through the Commons a manifesto declaring the petitioners to be 'enemies of the state'.

From that moment of gross provocation, relations between parliament and the new model became the motor of politics. In the remainder of the thirteen years of the civil wars they would time and again divide and weaken the Puritan cause. Finally they would destroy it. The issue bore no relation to the aims for which either parliament or its soldiers had gone to war.

By the summer of 1647 the new model had asserted its right to a say in the settlement of the kingdom. Fairfax, loyal to his men and loved by them, but no politician, yielded the political direction of the army to Cromwell, who turned to his son-in-law and fellow-officer Henry Ireton, the clearest political thinker within the army leadership, for the framing of constitutional proposals. Though Cromwell would often use force on parliaments to achieve political ends, he preferred to avoid it and to shun the stain of political illegitimacy that it was bound to bring. Now, resisting calls among the soldiers for a coup at Westminster, he strove, by a combination of threat and persuasion there, to whittle away Holles's majority and to bring the ascendancy to his own allies among the Independent MPs.

Even so he moved swiftly to secure and enlarge the military base of his power. A machinery of consultation was established, between senior and junior officers, and between junior officers and the ranks, which united the bulk of the army behind him. The minority of Presbyterians among the officers lost their authority over their troops, abandoned their commands in fear or despondency, and were replaced by men, mostly low-born, who were favoured by Cromwell. Delegates from the new model descended on the forces of the Presbyterian commander Sydenham Poyntz in the north, captured him, and removed him from his command. Bowing to those tactics, parliament extended Fairfax's commission to cover all the forces in England.

Cromwell acted so incisively in the spring and summer of 1647 because a new war was in prospect, this one within the parliamentarian cause. Holles was planning to create a counter-revolutionary army. He would recruit officers and soldiers from the outlying forces, from the Presbyterians in the new model, and from the groups of under-compensated former soldiers who were gathering resentfully and restlessly in London. Then there was the large and experienced militia of the City. It represented the mood among citizens who, horrified by the rise of the sects and by their challenges to social and religious discipline, were asserting the virtues of intolerant Presbyterians with growing conviction and resolve. Perhaps, too, Holles could draw in the Scots, those bitter enemies of the Independents. Yet Holles, like Charles I, always overplayed his hand. By July Cromwellian pressure at Westminster was working. Holles lost command of the Commons and, with ten of his allies, was impeached at the new model's instigation.

His defeat, however, provoked its own reaction. A mob of around 3,000 men invaded the Houses of Parliament in the Presbyterian cause. The Independent minority in both chambers, led by the Speakers, fled to the army, appealed to it for their restoration, and so gave it a legitimate ground to occupy the capital. When, early in August, the army duly marched on London, the opposition unexpectedly collapsed. Having reinstated the MPs, secured a purge of the City militia, and indicted a number of City politicians for treason, the new model withdrew in orderly fashion. Holles and his close allies went into exile. Yet he would soon be back, for the public sentiments on which he had played persisted. The struggle of Presbyterian and Independent, at Westminster, in the City, and in the provinces, would persist until the execution of the king.

Though the new model's dealings with parliament announced its political ambitions, it was in its relations with the king that the extent of them became clear. Again mistrust of the Presbyterians was the animating force. In early June, fearing that Holles intended to have Charles brought to London from Holdenby and restored to the throne, a small contingent of soldiers led by a cornet, George Joyce, seized the king and brought him to army headquarters at Newmarket. It was an improvised and muddled operation, conducted without Fairfax's knowledge and apparently exceeding the secret instructions of Cromwell, who seems to have wanted only to prevent a Presbyterian coup, not to transfer him into the army's hands. But once the new model had secured him it saw the political chance that his presence gave it. It treated him handsomely and, in conjunction with its allies at Westminster, offered him its own peace terms.

They were designedly more generous to him and his supporters than parliament's were. For would not the imposition of parliament's hard conditions, asked the army leaders, produce the Presbyterian domination of the king? Was not an intolerant Presbyterian Church as alarming a prospect as an intolerant episcopalian one? Was not 'new presbyter', as Milton had declared, 'but old priest writ large'? If only Charles would agree to liberty of worship for godly men outside the established Church, the army would allow him what parliament's negotiators had steadfastly refused him, the restoration of the bishops. The Book of Common Prayer, which parliament had outlawed, would also be preserved, again without compulsion, and the imposition of the Solemn League and Covenant would be revoked.

Charles's negotiations with the army in the summer of 1647 perhaps offered him his best chance of an honourable restoration. He spurned it. Convinced that none of the parties among his adversaries could prevail without his concurrence, he aimed to extract still more generous terms from the army, and then to use the concessions to draw yet more favourable ones from the English or Scottish Presbyterians.

The army's negotiating position, published in August as 'Heads of Proposals', brought a new perspective to the politics of the civil wars. Together with its provisions for liberty of conscience, the document carried a series of reform proposals which shifted attention away from the conflict of crown and parliament to wider concerns for the amelioration of society, for the communal responsibilities of its members, and for a revised relationship between government and subject.

Here as elsewhere the war had loosed forces which its instigators could not contain. High on the list of demands to emerge among the soldiers and their civilian supporters was the reform of parliamentary elections. In the pre-war era, when parliaments had met only occasionally and had had only limited powers, the geographical imbalances of parliamentary representation, created by what a later age would call rotten boroughs, had aroused few objections. But when, in the 1640s, the parliament in effect became the executive, and when it claimed to be fighting the war as the representative of the people, its unrepresentative character was exposed. The problem attracted further attention after parliament's decision to sanction a series of by-elections from 1645 to fill the seats left vacant by royalist MPs, a move which, while it did not much affect the overall balance of power in the Commons, did bring a number of radical figures, army officers among them, into the chamber. One of them was Henry Ireton. Though himself a beneficiary of electoral patronage, he resolved on its reduction and initiated a scheme for a wholesale redistribution of seats. The plan, launched by the Heads of Proposals, found widespread support in the ensuing years and was introduced in 1653, so that the two parliaments chosen while Cromwell was protector were elected on the basis of a reform as radical as that achieved, amid the different social pressures of the Industrial Revolution, by the Reform Act of 1832.

The Heads of Proposals also called for the redress of other grievances. Chiefly there were the geographically inequitable burden of taxation; the curbs imposed by the Long Parliament on the right of subjects to petition it; the trading monopolies held by mercantile oligarchies or granted by the crown to reward its friends and favourites; tithes, the system of compulsory payment by parishioners to their clergy; imprisonment, often in wretched conditions, for debt, a fate that deprived the debtors of the earnings from which they might make repayment; and the complexities and delays of legal proceedings, evils widely attributed to the self-interest of the lawyers, who were alleged to care more for their pockets than their clients.

The army's adoption of those issues reflected its image of itself as the champion of the people, whose liberties the parliament had ostensibly raised its forces to defend, but who in the soldiers' eyes had been betrayed by it. That self-perception grew in the spring and summer of 1647, when the new model's demands, which had initially centred on its own concerns for pay and indemnity, expanded under the influence of a mostly civilian group of writers and activists whom posterity knows as the Levellers, though the label, like others of the period, was disowned by those to whom it was applied. Themselves of urban or minor gentry back-grounds, they spoke particularly to the grievances of crafts-men and traders, especially in London, where their ideas spread before permeating the army.

The Leveller leaders were religious dissenters of one kind or another, though their demands were increasingly secular in tone and content. The most influential leader was John Lilburne, a self-publicist who had come to England's atten-tion as a victim of Laudian persecution, and whose histrionic prose turned his frequent imprisonments, under both monar-chical and parliamentarian rule, to martyrological advantage. The most accomplished writer among them was William Walwyn, the most provocatively subversive John Wildman, and the most penetrating Richard Overton, one of many Baptists who perhaps found in Leveller principles a political counterpart to the Baptist premise which, in matters of the spirit, repudiates imposed authority in favour of free consent.

There was much in the Leveller programme that the new model's leaders were willing to take up, but also much which alarmed them and in which they smelled republicanism and a threat to the security of property. Some Levellers argued that the ancient constitution, if it conflicted with natural and rational principles of government, should make way for them. Others appealed to images of Anglo-Saxon liberty, which had been crushed by the Norman Conquest and the aristocratic oppression it brought. Parliament had invoked the principle of the subject's representation at Westminster in order to claim ever wider powers for itself. The Levellers, by contrast, used it to demand restraints on parliamentary power. The legitimate authority of MPs, they argued, derived solely from the nation's consent and was 'inferior' to 'theirs who choose them'. No sovereign power, they maintained, could entrench on rights which the people 'reserved' to 'themselves'. The Levellers also developed arguments for an extension of the franchise, though they were uncertain whether the vote should be extended to all adult males. The issue had a peripheral place in their thinking, but when it was raised at army headquarters in October 1647 it provoked a discussion among officers and Levellers, the 'Putney debates', which was recorded in shorthand and which has startled modern readers by the democratic sentiments voiced in it.

Cromwell and Ireton were startled too. For the impact of the Levellers on the soldiers, which had initially worked to the advantage of the Cromwellians, had by the autumn come to threaten the new model's unity. Cromwell and Ireton were accused by their subordinates of selling out to the king in their negotiations with him, and of failing to insist on the army's demands for reform. In November a mutiny at Ware in Hertfordshire was vigorously suppressed, and the machinery of wide consultation and debate within the new model was terminated. The army's negotiations with Charles were abandoned too. During the Leveller agitation of November he escaped from Hampton Court, where the new model now held him, though when he reached the Isle of Wight the military governor, a friend of Cromwell whom the king had hoped to win over, incarcerated him again.

In December Charles was visited by emissaries from Scotland, to whom he pledged the establishment of Presbyterianism in England for a trial three-year period and the suppression of Independency and the sects. When the agreement, which made nonsense of his discussions with the parties in England, became known, it infuriated parliament and army alike, and gave them a renewed common cause. It also restored a semblance of unity in the new model. In January 1648 parliament resolved to negotiate with him no further. Yet if his own conduct weakened his position, there were movements at large which strengthened it, and which in 1648 brought a return to civil war.

The resurgence of royalism in the late 1640s, which drew in many men who had fought against him in the first war, owed nothing to the king's own conduct. The various groups among his followers watched with suspicion as he offered compromises now to one enemy, now to another. Yet majesty itself retained its awe, and Charles's own plight aroused compassion. On his journeys in captivity he was greeted by the acclamations of crowds and by the ringing of church bells. He stood for a lost world, one of 'halcyon days', which parliament and Puritanism had destroyed and which was now readily idealized. Religious feeling afforced the political reaction. The decade had produced a widespread destruction of images in churches and extensive purges of clergy who supported the king or who failed Puritan tests of pastoral care. The Directory of Worship, drawn up by the Westminster Assembly to replace the Prayer Book, had been published in 1645, and the legislative provisions for the Presbyterian system of Church government, launched in the same year, were completed in 1648.

Yet local sentiment and resourcefulness repeatedly thwarted the machinery of Puritan enforcement. A large proportion of non-Puritan ministers contrived to remain in their livings and to make at least some use of the Prayer Book. Puritan clergy who did replace Anglicans often found that their new parishioners refused them the payment of tithes. Some of the intruders reduced their already narrow base of support by barring from the sacrament parishioners who failed to manifest signs of divine grace. There was hunger for the popular festivities which the pre-war Church had condoned, and which came to symbolize a whole way of life that Puritanism was destroying. Riots against the suppression of Christmas, and the subsequent trial of some of the rioters, fanned the mood of protest that grew into renewed civil war in the spring and summer of 1648.

Nostalgia in Church and state was stoked by able propaganda. Defeated on the battlefield in 1642–6, royalism now won the battle of the pen. Parliament was unable to prevent, even in London, the appearance of newsbooks which used jaunty ballads and anti-Puritan satire in their bid to 'write his majesty back into his throne'. Before the war, parliament had suppressed the playhouses, more from a desire to prevent anti-Puritan gatherings than from principled hostility. But if plays could not be performed they could at least be printed, or reprinted. In volumes of plays, and of poems old and new, royalist editors and publishers saluted ideals of sociability and conviviality, and of honour and loyalty, which the sour parliamentarian cause was alleged to have wrecked. Wit and literary sophistication became badges of royalism. In return parliamentarians associated royalism with debauchery, excess, licentiousness.

Charles's defeat in the second civil war, as in the first, was not inevitable. He hoped for a conjunction between a Scottish invading force led by Hamilton and a series of local risings south of the border. He was helped by a mutiny in the fleet, of which a large component went over to him. Unlike the new model army, the navy had not been radicalized. It resented the recent dismissal, on Independent initiative, of its vice-admiral, Sir William Batten, whose sympathies were with the Presbyterian leaders at Westminster; and it took exception to his replacement by the radical soldier Thomas Rainsborough. The mutinous ships joined the Prince of Wales, the future Charles II, who had fled to exile in Holland and who now, around the time of his eighteenth birthday, led a fleet into the Thames.

The king lost the second civil war because Hamilton's army was delayed and reduced by divisions at Edinburgh; because, when it did invade, it was ineptly led and shockingly ill-disciplined; and because the new model responded rapidly and decisively, not only in confronting the Scots but in crushing or isolating the southern disturbances before they could spread through the land. The most serious risings were those in Kent, where the insurgents collaborated with Prince Charles's ships, and South Wales. Fairfax pursued the Kentish combatants into Essex and broke down the royalist resistance by laying siege to Colchester, which surrendered in August. His decision, after the siege, to have two of the royalist commanders executed indicates the intensity of feeling aroused by the war, a still more bitter contest than the first. In the same month Cromwell marched from Pembrokeshire to Lancashire, to confront Hamilton amid the mud and rain that drenched the combatants in the lanes and fields and moorland around the River Ribble close to Preston, where the Scots were decisively defeated.

Yet the second civil war, again like the first, solved nothing. Though parliament and army combined to win it, it reopened the division between them. The royalist reaction in the country weakened the hands of the radicals at Westminster and enabled the Presbyterians to recover their majority. They used it to resume negotiations with the king, which were opened at Newport in the Isle of Wight in September. In the army, by contrast, the war induced a profound shift of emotion. Anger and revulsion at the king's conduct merged with a sense of divine mission that was heightened by the new victories. The new model resolved to bring the king, 'that man of blood, to account for the blood he had shed'. While parliament's commissioners negotiated, the army drew up a *Remonstrance*, which it submitted to parliament on 20 November, calling for 'exemplary justice ... in capital punishment upon the principal author and some prime instruments of our late wars'.

The crisis came on 5 December, when the Commons, after a record sitting of almost twenty-four hours, resolved that concessions made by the king at Newport provided a basis for a settlement. It was the first favourable judgement the House had passed on any of Charles's offers. The terms were close to those he had rejected in 1646. Now that he had been defeated not once but twice, he had little alternative but to settle for them, as he did with a heavy and still duplicitous heart. Even after the return of the parliamentary commissioners to London he would have sown fresh confusion if he could. In the event, parliament itself was powerless to implement its agreement with him. In early December the army marched on London and had Charles moved to the mainland. Fairfax reluctantly led the forces into the capital, but in Cromwell's absence in the north it was with Ireton, who drafted the *Remonstrance*, that the initiative now lay. He intended to dissolve parliament by force, but friends among the minority in the Commons who opposed the peace terms persuaded him to purge it instead and to leave the MPs who had opposed the treaty in power.

Thus was there carried out, on 6 December and the days which followed, the operation known as Pride's Purge, after the commander, Colonel Thomas Pride, who executed it. Only members approved by the army were allowed into the Commons. The rest, if they risked trying to attend, were forcibly turned back. Of the 470 or so MPs qualified to sit before the purge, the coup permanently removed about 270. About a hundred more chose to stay away between the purge and the execution of the king on 30 January, and returned only afterwards.

If the membership of the Commons was radically reduced, the Lords, which would never have sanctioned the trial of the king, faced abolition. Its stance towards him had become increasingly cautious, and in 1648 it had refused even to declare the Scots who invaded on his behalf to be enemies. After Pride's Purge it raised scarcely a quorum. The remnant of the Commons – the Rump, as it would come to be contemptuously known – duly declared 'that the people are, under God, the original of all just power', and that their representatives in the Commons were thus entitled to act unilaterally. On that basis the Rump set up a High Court of Justice to try the king. One hundred and thirty-five parliamentarians, most of them MPs or soldiers or lawyers, were invited to sit as judges. Only about eighty attended the court when it met on 20 January, and only fifty-seven signed the death warrant.

Four weeks passed between Pride's Purge and the decision to set up the court. There are various possible reasons for the delay. Cromwell, who returned to London only when the purge was under way, would soon resume his leading role. He played the principal part in securing signatures to the death warrant. Yet while he was convinced that the trial was warrantable, he may for a time have questioned its prudence. It divided the army not merely from the Presbyterians but from a large body of its Independent friends, inside and outside parliament, whose support he was eager to retain, but who baulked at the killing of a king and at the mockery of parliamentary and legal procedures that secured it. Cromwell may even have hoped that Charles, whom the army transported from Hampshire to Windsor just before Christmas, might finally yield to terms acceptable to it, or agree to his own deposition and his replacement by his child, Henry Duke of Gloucester. It is conceivable, too, that Cromwell feared lest European powers, freed from the Thirty Years War by the Treaty of Westphalia in 1648, should intervene on the royalists' behalf. Or he may have hesitated to provoke the antagonism that Charles's death at English hands was bound to cause among his subjects in Ireland and Scotland.

Then there were the strains within the new model. The Levellers opposed the march on London in December. They wanted the army to commit itself to sweeping measures of social and parliamentary reform, and to the holding of fresh elections, before it seized power or removed the king. In

January the army held a series of internal debates before resolving on a reform programme which revived a number of the proposals of 1647, when the new model had likewise debated the settlement of the nation, and which was submitted to the Rump ten days before the regicide. It was called an *Agreement of the People*, the title that the Levellers had used for their own scheme for settlement in 1647.

Charles was executed both because of the strength of feeling in favour of his death and because of the belief, held by the army and its boldest allies at Westminster, that the peace and settlement of the nation, and the re-establishment of government, had become incompatible with his survival. Parallels drawn with the fate of tyrants of the Old Testament, and the conviction that God had marked out Charles for punishment, gave fervour to the proceedings against him and steeled the resolution of his judges and prosecutors. Yet they, like those who had made war on him in 1642, were wary of citing religious sanctions for their political deeds. The charge against Charles was secular in language. Before the war, it was alleged, he had pursued 'a wicked design to erect and uphold in himself an unlimited and tyrannical power to rule according to his will, and to overthrow the rights and liberties of the people'. Then he had 'traitorously and maliciously declared war' on his subjects.

In his demeanour at the trial Charles achieved a kind of greatness. His dignified refusal to accept the legality of the court or to enter a plea made nonsense of the proceedings against him. It also blocked any possibility of his reprieve. His execution was carried out on 30 January. On the scaffold, on a platform outside the Banqueting House, the building which Inigo Jones and Rubens had made a temple to kingship, he insisted on a principle by which he lived and died: that the liberty of the people consists in the rule of law, not in 'a share of the government', for 'a subject and a sovereign are clean different things'.

The regicide transformed the upheaval of which it was the climax. Most of the survivors among the MPs who had led the parliamentary attack on the crown's policies in 1640–2 had by now left Westminster, by wish or compulsion. The trial of the king had been unimaginable at the start of the first civil war and barely conceivable at its finish. Since the end of that war, Charles had told the parliamentarian factions that they could not manage without him. Now the army and its allies in parliament were about to meet that test. They could scarcely have been less well prepared for it.

4

REPUBLIC

❧⋅❦

Of the succession of governments which occupied power during the eleven years between the execution of Charles I and the return of his exiled son, none achieved a sense of legitimacy. All of them were improvised. All followed coups which had been recently or suddenly resolved on, and whose consequences had not been thought through. No one who had fought against the king in the civil war had had a kingless constitution in mind, and no one could find an enduring one now.

The Rump Parliament remained in power until 1653. In sanctioning the king's trial, and then overturning the ancient constitution, it claimed to act as the representative of a people which in reality neither was nor wished to be represented by it. MPs who had absented themselves from Westminster between Pride's Purge and the regicide were allowed to resume their seats on condition that they disown the vote, which had provoked the purge, in favour of restoring Charles on the Newport terms. Those who returned did so not from any enthusiasm for the new regime, but in order to moderate its course and to represent their constituents. Even after their return, however, attendances remained embarrassingly low.

The army, committed as it was to the principle of frequent parliamentary elections on a reformed electoral map, had pledged itself before the regicide to secure the rapid dissolution of the Long Parliament. Yet the new rulers encountered a problem that would plague the republic from start to finish. There was a general recognition that the defeated royalists must expect to be excluded from political participation for some space of time. To confine the electorate to voters sympathetic to the army and the regicide, however, it would have been necessary to go much further and to disenfranchise most parliamentarians. No parliament chosen on so narrow a base could have carried authority. When the army or the Levellers or the Rump spoke of 'the people' they meant the people who agreed with them, and whose judgements had not been perverted by enemy persuasion.

There was a small minority of politicians who, before the purge and the regicide, had begun to think about how to replace the king, but they had made little headway. Charles was tried not as a king but as a tyrant, who had deserted and betrayed the kingly office. Yet no alternative monarch was now to be found. The Stuarts would never have accepted their re-enthronement at the hands of the regicides. There were too many animosities within the new government for it even to consider agreeing on a candidate of its own, a solution that anyway would have been too radically at odds with parliament's professed war aims to command respect. England became a republic by default. Only in March did the Rump abolish the office of king, and then in ambiguous language. Only in May did it declare England to be a Commonwealth and Free State.

It was in March that it announced the abolition of the

House of Lords (though the Earls of Pembroke and Salisbury, England's most influential electoral magnates, would earn contempt inside and outside the peerage by standing successfully for the Commons in by-elections). In the preceding years some peers, notably the Earl of Essex and his rival the Earl of Northumberland, had assumed something of the air of medieval grandees. They seem to have thought of parliament merely as a temporary power base, and to have expected to dominate the government of the defeated king. Yet when there were clashes between Lords and Commons in the 1640s it was the Commons who won. The abolition of the Lords provoked far fewer protests then the ending of kingship.

At least the purged House of Commons constituted a government, which England had lacked since 1640 or 1642. Yet it was beleaguered on every side. Since the law ran in the king's name, the abolition of kingship created problems of legal as well as constitutional authority. Half the leading judges resigned. Charles's execution had made a martyr of him. His standing, and royalist sentiment, were enhanced by the posthumous appearance of a best-selling book in his name, *Eikon Basilike* (the 'king's book', as it came to be known), which vindicated the course of his reign.

Meanwhile the Presbyterian clergy issued furious protests, in print and pulpit, against the purge and the regicide. Only handfuls of civilian supporters of the new regime, most of them lacking local status, were ready to implement its will in the regions, though thousands of soldiers were on hand across the country to help them. The Rump, after a year of trying to impose its authority, decided to require its subjects to take a pledge of loyalty, an 'engagement', to the principle of government without king or Lords. The result was a bitter controversy which sharpened Presbyterian antagonism.

In the face of national hostility the army split still more dangerously than in 1647. Its *Agreement of the People* was quietly shelved. The Leveller leaders, incensed by the arbitrary power of the new government and of its executive body, the council of state, and concluding that the change from royal to parliamentary tyranny was 'a mere changing of persons', were imprisoned for their public protests. In May, anger at their incarceration helped to incite, in the area around Bristol, a major mutiny among the cavalry, which, as in 1647, was more receptive to Leveller ideas than the infantry. Only after a campaign which culminated in the capture of the ringleaders, and the execution of three of them, at Burford in Oxfordshire were Fairfax and Cromwell able to crush the revolt.

As a pressure group the Levellers were finished by the end of 1649, though political discontent would persist in the army through the next decade. Lilburne would twice persuade juries to acquit him, first in 1649 on a charge of treason, and then in 1653, when his defence of himself, against the charge of returning from the exile to which the Rump had condemned him the previous year, won him sympathy among the soldiery and a vocal public following. What the Levellers could not do was carry with them potential sympathizers, in and out of the army, who put godly reform and liberty of conscience before secular issues, and who, in pursuit of those goals, were prepared to stomach the constitutional irregularities of the 1650s.

Threats to the Rump at home were matched by challenges from abroad, where the regicide had an understandably chilly reception among Europe's princes. Ambassadors of the regime were assassinated by royalist refugees in Spain and Holland, whose rulers failed to meet the Commonwealth's demands that they bring the perpetrators to account. Charles II, as he moved in 1649–50 between Holland, France and Jersey, sought to mobilize Continental rulers on his behalf. In the Netherlands, which had just won its long-sought independence from Spain, the Stadtholder William of Orange, Charles's brother-in-law, who had succoured Charles's father in the civil war, sought an alliance with France that would restore the Stuarts and entrench William's own authority at home, where a republican party opposed it.

Henrietta Maria, no less politically active as queen mother than as queen, also looked for support to her native France, which had already dabbled, albeit to small effect, in the English politics of the civil war and its aftermath. Still fighting a major war against Spain, and now weakened by the Frondes, the French were unlikely to offer Charles II more than limited and indirect aid. But France did wink at piratical attacks from its ports on English merchant shipping. It also aided, together with Portugal, a royalist fleet commanded by Prince Rupert, who had turned – as some officers of the parliament's armies did – from landed campaigning to war at sea. His campaign of harassment against England's navy and merchant shipping, which took him to Ireland and the west African coast and America, endured until 1653.

It was to Ireland and to Scotland that Charles turned for more substantial assistance than the Continental powers were able or willing to grant him. On his father's death he was proclaimed king in both countries. The deposition of a ruler of three kingdoms was bound to have transforming consequences in all of them – as the men who removed Charles I's second son James from the throne forty winters later would likewise discover. Despite the failure of Denzil Holles to get new model regiments sent to Ireland in 1647, the intervening two years had brought the parliamentarians some gains there. The Protestant Marquis of Ormonde, who had sustained Charles I's cause in Ireland but had been left powerless by the king's defeat in England, had surrendered to parliament in 1647 in the service of the anti-Catholic struggle, the cause that to his mind should have held royalists and parliamentarians together. In 1648 the Catholic Confederacy, more torn than ever between those who put loyalty to the king first and the clerical and papal party which saw in the conflict in England a chance to claim Ireland for the Counter-Reformation, went to war with itself. But in the same year the second civil war in England, and the prospect of the regicide, brought altered perspectives. A fortnight before the king's execution Ormond signed a treaty with the Confederates which raised the prospect of combined action against the parliament.

Within England the regicide brought a sense of deracination not only to politics but to society at large. Though most responses to the event were either angry or melancholy, in some quarters the punishment of God's anointed, and the ensuing constitutional changes, wrought a heady excitement. New religious sects, bold and strident, emerged. The Fifth Monarchy men converted the millenarian speculation which was common among Puritans, but which drew back from confident prophecy about the divine timetable for the end of the world, into a certainty that the reign of Christ's saints on earth was imminent. Rightful power, they maintained, lay not with elected parliaments but with themselves, who as

God's elect would subjugate the wicked. Unlike other sects they acquired a direct influence on the course of events, thanks particularly to the leadership of the MP and army officer Thomas Harrison.

Then there were the Diggers, or True Levellers as they were ready to name themselves. Inspired by the gifted pamphleteer Gerrard Winstanley, they asserted that Adam's fall would be reversed, and each soul brought to God, by the abolition of property and human servitude. Proceeding beyond pamphleteering to social action, they set up a commune in Surrey, dedicated to the common ownership of the fruits of the earth. The army, having initially judged the experiment harmless, destroyed it on the orders of the council of state. Perhaps most startling of all were the people, derisively called Ranters, who maintained that their bond with God freed them from moral laws, though it is hard to know how much the more colourful accounts of their conduct, which reported women stripping naked in church or claiming to have been impregnated by the deity, owed to the blackening intent of the adversaries who publicized them. Behind all those movements there lay the often perplexed, often despairing, often ecstatic spiritual sojourns of men and women seeking their salvation in an age of institutional breakdown and collapsing certainties.

The most dynamic, the largest, and the most enduring of the new groups was the last to emerge, the Quakers, a body very different from the sober-spirited pacifist organization that they became in later ages. From 1652, inspired by George Fox, bands of Quakers resolved to awaken the world to the inner light of the spirit, which in their thinking transcended theological speculations and the historical record of the Bible. To that end they roamed England, interrupting church services, haranguing clergy or challenging them to debate, and refusing conventional marks of social respect, most controversially the raising of hats, which the Diggers had also gainsaid. An avalanche of pamphlets supported Quaker agitation. The panic that the Quakers could provoke would be most vividly illustrated in 1656, when James Nayler, a leading figure in the movement, was brought before an outraged parliament on a charge of blasphemy after riding into Bristol on a donkey in imitation of Christ's entry into Jerusalem. Though calls for the death penalty were defeated, he suffered severe physical punishment.

Political thinking was deracinated too. Now that the ancient constitution had collapsed, arguments about the correct balance of power within it, which had exercised writers of the 1640s, were redundant. Instead the sway of the sword produced meditations on raw facts of power. Thomas Hobbes's *Leviathan* in 1651 insisted that subjects owe obedience to any government, good or bad, which gives them protection. His thesis echoed pamphlets which the Rump itself had sanctioned, bereft as the government was of more uplifting arguments that might reconcile the nation to its rule. Hobbes's book mirrors, too, the 'Horatian Ode' of the former royalist Andrew Marvell in 1650, the greatest political poem of the civil wars, which, even as it laments the execution of Charles I, who 'nothing common did or mean | Upon that memorable scene', acknowledges the irrecoverable loss of the 'ancient rights' of king and constitution, which 'hold or break | As men are strong or weak'.

*

In August 1649 Cromwell, hitherto preoccupied with the politics of the new regime, of which he was the most powerful member, led an army to Ireland, of which parliament had made him lord lieutenant. Arriving late in the campaigning season, he resolved on swift action. His victories at the eastern coastal towns of Drogheda and Wexford are notorious for his brutal treatment of the enemy, which conformed to the *mores* of the war in Ireland, but which has been viewed with outrage there since the rise of Irish nationalism in the nineteenth century. At Drogheda his men drove royalist soldiers into a church steeple and set light to the pews beneath. Those who got out alive were put to the sword. More than 300 soldiers on the Irish side were executed after the fighting had finished. Cromwell's conduct was warrantable by the conventions of warfare, for the enemy had refused the offer of quarter. But behind it there lay a ferocious biblical and anti-Catholic zeal, and an assurance that his ruthlessness was divine retribution for the massacre of 1641.

At least he succeeded, by the example of terror, in reducing subsequent bloodshed. The back of the resistance had been broken by the end of the winter, and in 1650 what remained of it fell apart. The Catholic bishops rounded on Ormonde and excommunicated him. Yet only in 1652 did the English army complete the conquest of Ireland. It did so at a terrible cost to the conquered, for the victorious troops brought with them disease which, together with the fighting, has been estimated to have wiped out a fifth of the native population. There was starvation too. Holders of small properties were driven from their land into the wilds and often into banditry.

Cromwell himself returned to England in May 1650 to

lead a force into Scotland, the focus of Charles II's hopes after the failure of the Irish resistance. Fortunately for the republic, revulsion at the regicide could not unite the Scots. Montrose led a failed rising on the king's behalf against the Presbyterian regime and was executed in the month of Cromwell's return to England. The fortunes of the exiled king were low. He had rejected the advice which Edward Hyde had also given to Charles I, and which was resisted now as then by Henrietta Maria, as divisive a figure at her son's court as she had been at her husband's. Hyde believed that the Puritans would never create a lasting government, and that the crown would be wise to stick to its political and ecclesiastical principles and to seek support only among their adherents. Instead Charles was ready to follow his mother's advice and, more brazenly than his father, to make concessions to Presbyterians or Catholics, whatever the offence given to his Anglican following.

In Scotland, Montrose's defeat drove the king into Presbyterian hands. Charles sailed there in June 1650, renounced his Irish and Catholic supporters, and acknowledged his father's sinfulness in refusing the Covenant. The republic resolved on a pre-emptive invasion. Fairfax, believing it unjustified, resigned as lord general and was replaced by Cromwell. Now confronted by a Protestant enemy, Cromwell used gentler means than in Ireland. Yet the challenge to his invading army was formidable. In September, outmanoeuvred by the Scottish general David Leslie, it found itself hemmed in at Dunbar, on the coast east of Edinburgh. If Cromwell had lost the ensuing battle, England would have lain open to the Scots and to the restoration of the monarchy at their hands. His victory, won against heavy odds, had an impact on his army's sense of identity and mission as significant as those of the earlier triumphs at Naseby and Preston. It brought a dizzying consciousness of divine favour, and intensified the conviction of the soldiers that they were entitled to a say in England's post-war settlement.

Dunbar sowed fresh divisions among the defeated Scots. Even so Cromwell found it impossible, during the arduous campaign over the following year, to bring them to a decisive battle. Eventually, reckoning shrewdly that the English disliked Scotsmen still more than they did the Rump, he tempted the Scots into undertaking their third invasion of England in the period, and pursued them from the rear. In September 1651 the Scottish army, having roused little support in England, was destroyed at Worcester. Charles, who had headed it, escaped to resume his vagrant exile.

In all three kingdoms the royalist cause was now lost. In England conspirators remained, but they were divided along the lines of the exiled court, and their communications with it were penetrated by the intelligence system established under the Rump by the MP Thomas Scot and later developed by John Thurloe, Cromwell's secretary of state. Many royalists resigned themselves to submission. Royalist literature, which in the late 1640s had offered solace to the victims of Puritan supremacy but had also incited resistance to it, now rarely ventured beyond its consolatory purpose. Izaak Walton's *The Compleat Angler*, one of its high achievements in the 1650s, pays homage to rural retreat.

What would the Rump and its army do with their new-found power? Within parliament there were two opposing impulses. On one hand was the desire to entrench the new regime: to commemorate the anniversaries of the regicide, to extirpate the remnants of monarchical rule, and to restrict the membership of central and local government to men ready to pledge allegiance to the Commonwealth. On the other there was the wish to heal the nation's wounds, to relegate the regicide to the past, and to rebuild at least part of the broader parliamentarian and Puritan party. The second of those impulses commanded a majority in the Commons. Yet the first tendency had two strengths. First, in general it had the army behind it. Secondly, the new regime was unlikely to acquire confidence or authority without establishing a distinctive identity to contrast it with the old one.

The initiative accordingly lay with men who had achieved the coup of 1649. Their most powerful representatives among the civilians at the heart of government were the intelligence chief Thomas Scot of Buckinghamshire and the lawyer John Bradshaw of Cheshire, who had presided over the king's trial, and who, although not a member of parliament, was president of its council of state. The values of this party were proclaimed by Bradshaw's friend Milton, who during the civil wars set poetry aside for polemical prose, and whom the council made Secretary for Foreign Tongues. Although Milton's reply to *Eikon Basilike* in 1649, *Eikonoklastes*, failed to match the impact of the work it attacked, he had a literary triumph in 1651 with a Latin vindication of the regicide, *Defensio*, which echoed across Europe.

In 1649–51, when the royalist challenge persisted, the two tendencies lived in uneasy coexistence. In the wake of Dunbar the Rump conceded to the army two measures – 'acts', as the self-proclaimed sovereign power now termed its legislation. They were on the subjects on which the new model's reforming aspirations had come mainly to focus: the law and the Church. Legal proceedings were henceforth to be held, not in the specialized Norman French which bewildered clients, but in English. Secondly, there was legislation to end the compulsory attendance of 'pious and peaceably minded' people at services of the established Church, so long as they attended alternative places of worship on Sundays. Even before Dunbar, Harrison had secured another victory of legislation in religion, the appointment of a commission which established and financed a system of itinerant preaching by sectaries in Wales, a land notoriously resistant to Puritan understandings of God's word. Yet initiatives for reform encountered stiff resistance in the Commons. In the case of legal reform it came from lawyers, a tight and numerous pressure group in the chamber. In the case of religion it came from MPs alarmed by the boldness of the sects and anxious to reassure conventional Puritan opinion. Severe laws, of the kind which Presbyterians had urged before Pride's Purge, were passed against adultery and incest, and attempts to abolish the admittedly ineffective Presbyterian Church were seen off.

What, amid those controversies, of Cromwell? He was fifty-two at the time of Worcester. Though he remained lord general, the victory ended his career on the battlefield. He returned to Westminster, where his presence overshadowed the debates. Yet, to his frustration, he could not control them. He aimed to reconcile or balance the two competing impulses at the centre of power, a policy that earned him mistrust from both sides. His influence depended on the unity of the army and on its loyalty to him. Yet he strove to restrain its political demands. He wanted to reconcile the nation to the new order. A reformer but not a revolutionary, he strove to make England a land fit for God's eyes, but with its institutions and social structure essentially intact. He preferred, not to assail interest groups which opposed reform, but to secure their cooperation. In the months after Worcester he persuaded parliament to commission experts who, in the spheres of Church and law, would draw up substantial but essentially moderate reforms. They proved too substantial for the Rump's liking, too moderate for the radicals inside and outside the army.

Changes in the Church were designed under the leadership of his chaplain John Owen, now the most prominent of the Independent divines. Alterations in legal procedures were drawn up by a body chaired by a judge, a former royalist, Matthew Hale. Owen's scheme was the more contentious. It provided for the continuing interdependence of Church and state, which would unite to control the composition of the clergy and to define doctrinal orthodoxy. Within those limits, but only within them, it guaranteed liberty of conscience. Since the removal of the Presbyterians from power, the alliance of their common enemies, the Independents and sectaries, had dissolved. Scarcely less than the Presbyterians, Owen took exception to the new sects of the 1650s. He was dismayed by the approach of some of them to the Bible, whose literal meaning and historical content got lost, as he saw it, in their loose and fancifully allegorical interpretations. Cromwell was troubled by it too. He offended the radicals not only by his support for Owen but by refusing to give more than notional support to the increasingly belligerent movement for the abolition of tithes.

The Rump declined to take its agenda from Cromwell or the army, and stalled over the Hale and Owen schemes. It had ambitious, indeed visionary, programmes of its own, to which the civilian radicals gave more attention than to the issues of law and religion. Their goal, pursued with high energy and ability and with the weapons, military and administrative, which civil war had fashioned, turned outward from the native preoccupations that had divided king and parliament. MPs looked to the greatening of the nation's power and wealth, which the new rulers hoped would win over the country to the new government.

England's conquest of Ireland and Scotland had been ably backed, as the new model's earlier exploits had been, from Whitehall. It was followed by innovative legislation to reconfigure the relations of the three countries, to England's advantage. Ireland and Scotland were 'incorporated' into the English Commonwealth, on terms which weakened their national identities and institutions, and which included their representation in English parliaments. Thirty MPs for Ireland, and thirty for Scotland, would accordingly be returned in the elections of the 1650s, though, given the dependence of English supremacy in both countries on military occupation, it is not surprising that many of them were nominees, and a number of them members, of the occupying regimes.

There was a still bolder initiative for a union of nations. Under the early Stuarts, England had cut an unimpressive figure on the Continent. In the 1650s its standing was transformed. Puritans had long wanted an anti-Spanish foreign policy. Yet even the most belligerent ideological postures can yield to facts of power and diplomacy. The Rump, though it did not openly befriend Spain, leant towards it. Portugal and the Netherlands, which had won independence from Spain in the 1640s, remained hostile to their former master. So when the Portuguese aided Prince Rupert, and when the House of Orange succoured Charles II, Spain resolved to give diplomatic recognition, as its rival France had not, to the English republic. The Dutch, who had won their war of independence against Spain in 1648, and whose trade now flourished in that hard-won peace, were the Commonwealth's principal diplomatic concern. The Rump urged them to renounce the semi-sovereignty of the Orange dynasty and to form an alliance with England. Early in 1651 an embassy to Holland, led by Oliver St John, secretly carried with it a sensational proposal: the full integration, or something like it, of the two new republics.

Behind that daring scheme lay the realization that the countries could share military, naval and commercial resources that would defy any monarch. Improbable as the proposal seems in retrospect, it gained credence at the time from the precariousness of the Dutch republic, a body which was too decentralized for effective political coordination, and from the suspicion that it could not survive as an independent state. But English feelings about the Dutch, fellow-Protestants but economic rivals, had always been ambivalent. When the Dutch turned the proposed union down, St John indignantly returned to England and persuaded parliament to pass a protectionist Navigation Act, aimed mainly at the Dutch, which restricted the import of goods into England to English ships or ships from the country of origin.

The Navigation Act, which had wide support in the merchant community, was only the most assertive of a range of measures intended to improve England's commercial prowess at its neighbours' expense. Within that community, Pride's Purge and the regicide had altered the balance of power. The oligarchy that had previously run the City, and had collaborated with parliament in the 1640s, consisted largely of members of the Levant and East India Companies, which were state-backed monopolies. For decades a number of enterprising merchants, many of them of lower social background then the monopolists, had chafed at their exclusion from that privileged circle. They had broken illicitly into the companies' trade to the east, while also commandeering much of the commercial exchange with the emerging American colonies, to which the monopolies did not extend. A group of them, headed by Maurice Thomson, had formed close links with the new model and with the Independent congregations in the City. In 1641 a revision of the rules controlling elections to the City government had enabled John Pym to capture the City for parliament. After Pride's Purge another such revision gave control of it to the army's allies.

The circle around the ubiquitous Thomson took its part in the outburst of creative commercial energy that marks the rule of the Commonwealth. It worked with a group of merchant MPs whose close cooperation, and whose commercial knowledge, gave them an influence on economic policy disproportionate to their numbers. In 1650 the Rump set up a council to foster new initiatives in trade and manufacture, and passed legislation to cripple the trade of those English colonies in North America and the Caribbean where royalists were obstructing the acceptance of the new regime. One idea, taken up by advocates of a close alliance with the Netherlands, was to attract trade to England by freeing the ports from customs dues, though the breakdown of relations with the Dutch put paid to it. In the commercial initiatives of the early 1650s, and in the flexing of the Commonwealth's muscles in its relations with its neighbours, the joint pursuits of gain and godliness produced, in devout and hard-headed merchants and in idealist thinkers, intoxicating visions of a newly prosperous society whose wealth, no less than the might of the army and navy of the infant Commonwealth, would be an instrument for the Puritanization of Europe.

The civil wars were already a fertile period in the devising and publication of proposals for commercial and agricultural innovation. They owed much to the coordinating activities of the Polish émigré Samuel Hartlib, who in due course would work in the office of Cromwell's secretary of state. With friends of international experience and background, who like him had first-hand knowledge of the horrors of the Thirty Years War, he looked to England to achieve the unification of European Protestantism. Yet his idealism could clash with facts of power. The Dutch war ran counter to his pan-Protestant aspirations, while his proposals for state-sponsored encouragement for the diffusion of practical scientific knowledge could not compete with the urgent demands of political and financial survival that pressed on all the governments of the 1650s.

What made the Navigation Act largely enforceable was the strengthening of the navy, where the royalist sympathies that had divided the fleet in 1648 had been eliminated. The Admiral, the Earl of Warwick, had adhered to the parliamentarian cause during the naval mutiny of 1648. Of the political leaders among the peers he was the one least unsympathetic to the governments of the decade after the regicide. But the Commonwealth did not trust him. In 1649 it transferred control of the navy to a committee of radical MPs, overhauled the composition of the naval officers, and began a zealous process of administrative reform. During the Rump's rule a massive, and massively ambitious, programme of shipbuilding in the dockyards of Kent nearly quadrupled the number of the state's warships, and gave the Commonwealth a force at sea that no Continental power could hope to match.

Squadrons roamed European waters and the routes to America, and extinguished the royalist bases, which had damaged England's coastal and international trade, in the Scilly Isles and the Channel Islands. Naval convoys protected commerce from pirates in northern Europe and in the Mediterranean, a system that would be extended later in the decade. In 1650 a Commonwealth fleet under Admiral Blake cowed Portugal, and ended the Portuguese support for Rupert, by attacking that nation's returning Brazilian fleet as it entered the River Tagus. France paid for its hostility to the Commonwealth in 1652, when Blake shattered a French fleet that was besieging the Spanish-controlled port of Dunkirk, that nest of anti-English piracy.

Scarcely less imposing was the naval expedition to the New World led by Sir George Ayscue in 1651–2. It brought Virginia and Barbados, which had revolted after the regicide, under parliamentarian control. The civil wars had loosened the ties between England and its colonies, which neither king nor parliament had had the resources to command. The end of Laudianism had stemmed the flow of emigration to the New World; indeed some colonists returned from New England to support parliament's cause. Most of those who stayed in America hoped to keep their new lands free of the civil wars and its allegiances. Yet there were too many connections with the homeland, personal and institutional, for the colonial governments to escape varying degrees of polarization and contention, which damaged trade and public order. Royalist exiles arrived to animate discontent, and played on the colonists' resentment at the Rump's aim to restrict the freedom of their trade to England's advantage. In formulating that policy the Rump became the first regime to conceive something like a general policy for the colonies, though neither it nor the succeeding governments of the 1650s could reverse the development of the colonies' own identities.

It was in nearer waters that the Commonwealth's policies were most ambitious and successful. Charles I had ineffectively resolved to assert England's sovereignty over England's neighbouring seas. The Rump asserted it effectively, and by doing so affronted the Dutch no less than by the Navigation Act. It was the refusal of Dutch ships to strike sail to English ones in the Channel that sparked the outbreak of war between the two nations in July 1652, the first of three major Anglo-Dutch naval wars of the seventeenth century, which in their scale drew comparisons with the conflict of Rome and Carthage. In 1652 the advantage lay with the Dutch, who humiliated the English navy at Dungeness in November. The disaster provoked another overhaul of naval administration. It bore fruit in an epic English victory off Portland in February 1653, which altered the balance of the war.

Cromwell, thwarted by the Rump over domestic policy, was defeated over foreign policy too. He held to the conventional Puritan preference for a Protestant alliance against Spain, though with his old ally Sir Henry Vane, who was a leading member of the Rump and the dominant figure of its naval administration, and who also regretted the Anglo-Dutch war, he did his best to help England win it. The mountainous expense of the war, which the Rump met partly by a fresh swathe of land confiscations from royalists,

damaged Cromwell's efforts to secure the pardon and reconciliation of those of the king's supporters who were willing
to live quietly under the republic.

Already the monthly assessment had been raised to the
sum, huge even by the standards of wartime taxation, of
£120,000. The military budget was enormous, for the Irish
and Scottish campaigns, and the military occupation of
England that alone kept the population in check, had
increased the army to around 70,000 men, almost three
times the size of the new model in 1648, when in turn it
had more or less doubled in numbers since the last stages
of the first war. Everyone in government agreed that it
would have to be reduced. Yet large forces were needed
to hold the three nations down, and especially for the
occupation of Ireland and Scotland. Besides, the prospect
of even partial disbandment under parliamentary orders
revived memories in the army of parliament's treatment of
it in 1647. Though a number of soldiers were redeployed
into the naval service during the Dutch war, that conflict
was fought without the army's approval and stole some of
its thunder.

For the Rump, which had been brought into being by the
army, scarcely had more love for it than the parliament had
had before Pride's Purge. After the regicide the Commons
had pointedly refused to appoint the MPs and army officers
Ireton and Harrison, who had been heavily involved in the
purge, to the council of state. From August 1652 relations
between parliament and army deteriorated rapidly. That
was partly because the Rump, burdened by its administrative and naval undertakings, had got seriously behind
with its legislative business; partly because of its insistence,
no less keen than that of the Presbyterians in 1647, that

the army was the mere servant of parliament; and partly because of its resistance to the army's reform programme, a stance highlighted by parliament's unwillingness, which caused intense ill-feeling among the sectaries, to renew the commission for the evangelization of Wales.

It was also because of the Rump's prolongation of its power. In the 1650s as in the 1640s, MPs agreed that there should be parliamentary elections at fixed intervals. The Rump drafted legislation for biennial parliaments, but roused suspicion in the army by delaying the passage of it. Was not the parliament, which had sat since 1640, clinging to office from self-interest? When taxation was so high, and when so many demands for financial redress – for repayment to lenders to the parliamentarian war effort, or for assistance to soldiers and civilians to whom the war had brought lasting suffering – went unanswered, the cry went up that MPs were pocketing government revenue or helping themselves to the confiscated estates of the crown and royalists and the Church (though army officers themselves speculated extensively in land purchases). Similar accusations had been levelled at parliament in the years before Pride's Purge.

Were the charges fair? Some financial irregularities were perhaps inevitable in an age when the remuneration of politicians depended more on perquisites than on salaries, even if the levels of taxation in the 1650s facilitated something of a shift towards a salary system. Many of England's new rulers had themselves contributed extensively to the war effort at costs to their own pockets, and looked to compensate themselves. Inside knowledge enabled some of them to head the queues for bargains in land sales. Yet there were too many rivalries among the parliamentarian MPs, who watched each other's transactions closely, for peculation to become rife. Contractors who provided the supplies of warfare, or who collected the state's revenue, seem occasionally to have abused the system, possibly with the collusion of politicians. In general, however, the financial needs of the parliamentarian cause impelled its leaders to drive hard bargains with the contractors and to hold them to account. Some parliamentarian and military leaders made fortunes from the wars, though not immense ones. A few built country houses with their gains. But there was no social takeover by a victorious political class.

It was the Rump's reluctance to dissolve that gave the antagonism of parliament and army its focus. From the soldiers and the radical congregations came mounting pressure on Cromwell to expel the parliament by force. Yet there was a familiar contradiction in the army's position, which its indignation at the Rump's conduct obscured from it, but which was exposed when, in 1653, parliament changed its stand. It decided that fresh elections, whatever the risk they carried, were the only means of curbing the army's political assertiveness and of restoring a measure of constitutional legitimacy to civilian rule.

Its decision was incorporated into an electoral bill which, while it would have excluded royalists from the vote, would have given it to Presbyterians, whose representatives at Westminster had been purged in December 1648. It was to prevent the passage of the bill that on 20 April Cromwell led a file of musketeers into the chamber, railed at the moral depravity of the members, forcibly cleared the chamber, and declared the parliament dissolved. The army, having in 1649 destroyed one of the two sides in the civil war, had now dispatched the other.

*

How would it replace it? The army's succession of military victories, which had confounded so much human calculation and had demonstrated God's liking for working his wonders in defiance of it, had instilled in Cromwell and his circle a mistrust of political planning. If God's servants were true to his purposes, they were sure, the Lord would provide.

In Cromwell's mind there were, however, limits to God's revolutionary intent. In the aftermath of the coup of April 1653, as of that of January 1649, the lord general strove to contain the radical impulses he had unleashed. Harrison, the Fifth Monarchist, wanted government by an assembly of seventy fellow-sympathizers, to be modelled on the Sanhedrin of the Old Testament. Cromwell took up the idea and subtly modified it. The army would choose an assembly of its friends, but it would be twice the size envisaged by Harrison; it would have a broader political base; and it would have only interim power. He wanted the gathering to push through the reforming legislation which the Rump had resisted. Those measures, he hoped, would help win over the electorate to Puritanism, and thus pave the way for elections, which he hoped to hold by 1655.

On the premise that, as lord general of the army which the parliament had appointed, he represented the nearest thing to a legitimate power, Cromwell took it on himself to summon the nominated members to Whitehall on 4 July. They sat thereafter in the Commons' chamber, and resolved to call themselves a parliament. In retrospect he would describe the assembly as 'a tale of my own weakness and folly'. The reforms of Church and law which had been designed by Owen and Hale at his behest, and which the

Rump had rejected as too far-reaching, were judged by the new parliament to be not extensive enough. Its members, who on average were of lower social status than the normal membership of the Commons, were derisively known as 'Barebone's Parliament' after one of its members, the Puritanically named leather seller and lay preacher Praise-God Barebone.

Even a parliament hand-picked by the army managed to provoke it, not least by a proposal that the senior officers aid the reduction of the state's debts by forgoing their pay for a year. Yet it was the radicalism of the reform programme of the majority that brought the assembly's downfall. Barebone's resolved to abolish the Court of Chancery, a bedrock of the legal system and of the security of landed property, and then decided on the abolition of tithes, in whose preservation not only the clergy, but the people and institutions that owned parish livings, had a financial interest. The horror and panic provoked by those steps threatened to destroy the Puritan cause. On 12 December Barebone's was dissolved by yet another army coup.

Four days later, in a low-key ceremony, Cromwell was installed as Lord Protector. He ruled by virtue of a written constitution, drawn up mainly by army officers, the Instrument of Government. Having kept, through the period of the Rump and Barebone's, to the rule of sovereign parliaments, the army leaders now abandoned it and returned to the old division between executive and legislature. The provisions of the Instrument were close to those which the army had offered Charles I in 1647, but with a protector in the king's place. There were to be triennial parliaments, each of limited duration. Liberty of conscience for the godly was guaranteed.

The elevation of Cromwell had long been predicted. His enemies now accused him of having plotted it all along. He was accused, too, of enjoying the grandeur of power in the sober but stately and costly court which the protectorate established at Whitehall and Hampton Court. Among the groups which had exercised power from 1649 to 1653 there was outrage at his seizure of it. The grandees of the Rump period, Scot, Bradshaw, Vane and the former civil-war commander Sir Arthur Hesilrige, conspired or protested against the protectorate. Even St John, Cromwell's cousin, kept at arm's length from it. There was disaffection in the army, the navy, and the City. Throughout the protectorate Cromwell would hear the allegation, which grieved him, that he had sacrificed the causes of godliness and liberty, for which parliamentarians had fought, to his ambition. In reply, he and his spokesmen could point out that he had declined the offer, which the Instrument contained, of the title of king; that his powers were curbed by the constitutional restraints which the Instrument allocated both to parliament and to an executive council; and that the new constitution provided not for hereditary rule, which would have produced a Cromwellian dynasty, but for election by the council.

Cromwell, who wanted the advantages of single rule but not the opprobrium of having acquired it, portrayed himself as half a king, under whom the republic half survived. To his mind, forms of government, and their trappings, were of little moment, save as they served or obstructed his overriding aims of godly reformation and liberty of conscience. Those goals, he judged, might be more readily attainable under a form closer to tradition than the regimes of 1649–53. A number of religious dissenters agreed, and looked to the Instrument as the 'Magna Carta' of religion.

Yet the principle of parliament's supremacy, which had been hurriedly adopted in the emergency of 1649, had subsequently won many converts, especially among men who bore the heat and burden of exercising it. Some thinkers urged, as a healthy alternative to single rule, the creation of republican institutions parallel to those of classical antiquity, an ideal that, with the blessing of the radical party in the Rump, was brought to a wide readership in editorials of weekly newsbooks of the early 1650s by Marchamont Nedham. Most of the hostility to single government in the 1650s, however, was less intellectually speculative. Wary of new constitutional architecture, its exponents clung to the principle of unicameral rule: to the undivided sovereignty of the Commons, the remnant of the old constitution.

A number of influences induced or heightened anti-monarchical feeling: the military and naval triumphs of the republic, which surpassed the feats of any English king; the sense that God had cast down monarchy and its 'lordly' power; the recognition that the republic, to survive, needed its own ideological momentum; and, from 1653, the resentment at Cromwell's usurpation by the men he had usurped. Advocates of parliamentary supremacy who opposed the protectorate called themselves 'commonwealthsmen'. A number of army officers and former members of the Rump suspended their differences, not for the last time, in the anti-Cromwellian cause, and conspired, impotently as it proved, for his overthrow. A handful plotted with royalists, on the principle that if there had to be a single ruler it should be the legitimate one.

Cromwell's role in the civil wars has often been

exaggerated, both by historians and in popular memory, which sometimes confuses his deeds with those of his ancestor Thomas Cromwell, the hammer of the monks, and which has Oliver fighting or sleeping in many a village which saw other parliamentarian soldiers but which he never visited. For the first half of the civil war, when chance largely confined him to the military corridor between Yorkshire and the Eastern Association, he played a valuable but secondary role. Yet, as often happens, a reaction against historical exaggeration has swung towards the opposite extreme. His role in the training and disciplining of parliament's crack regiments, and his exploits at Marston Moor and Naseby, were decisive. His later victories, inside and outside England, were still more remarkable. Through them, but also through willpower and political dexterity, a provincial gentleman-farmer, an obscure figure until his forties, rose to conquer three nations and to awe the courts of Europe.

As protector, Cromwell sought to reduce the political temperature and restore a sense of stability. The Rump's 'engagement' was quickly repealed. Parliamentary elections in 1654 and 1656 brought back into politics MPs who had not sat since Pride's Purge. Always averse to ideological rigidity, he promoted malleable men, some of them ex-royalists, to office. Of the twenty men who sat on the executive council of the protectorate, none had been regicides.

He was in favour of flexibility on other fronts too. With intermittent exceptions he tacitly permitted private Anglican worship. He knew that his regime would never win national acceptance so long as Anglican sentiment remained hostile to it. He also knew that, alongside the defiantly royalist leaders among the Anglican clergy, there were divines who were asking themselves whether the link between Church and monarchy need be inseparable. Dismayed by the readiness of both Charles I and Charles II to treat with Presbyterians and Catholics at Anglicanism's expense, they contemplated accommodation with the new order. If the Church were to disown the Stuarts and abandon its claim to a monopoly of worship, might not a deal with Cromwell end the darkness of proscription? There are hints that the protector, who had been willing to restore bishops in 1647, continued to envisage a place for a modified system of episcopacy within a Puritan ecclesiastical settlement, though the attempts at negotiation got nowhere. Catholics, too, benefited from his political realism. At the outset of the civil wars he had been fiercely hostile to English Catholics. That passion had cooled, in him and in others. Catholics were now mainly left alone by the competing Puritan groups, which vented their ire on each other, though a measure passed by parliament in 1656, requiring Catholics to abjure the claims of the papacy to their loyalty, would have given a new spur to anti-Catholicism if it had been widely enforced.

Cromwell, however, had lost none of his resolve to Puritanize and reform the land, and to effect the changes in Church and law that he had urged on the Rump and Barebone's. Over law reform, which, in the moderate guise in which he commended it, he hoped would win the support of property owners vexed by arcane legal processes, he was able to get only minor changes past the resourceful resistance of the legal profession. In religion he achieved more. The parliamentarians had devoted much energy and enterprise to the replacement of unsatisfactory clergy and to the improvement, largely from the yield of confiscated lands, of the income of impoverished livings, though the achievement was patchy. Cromwell brought order to those processes. He took pride in the creation of two bodies, the 'triers', who vetted candidates for livings, and the 'ejectors', who evicted unsatisfactory ministers. The programme of ejection, like so much Puritan reform, was undermined by local opposition and inertia, but the triers, a broadly based Puritan group, seem to have done much to improve, by Puritan lights, the quality of the clergy.

So do Cromwell's exertions as Lord Chancellor of Oxford University, the training ground, with Cambridge, of the clergy, as also of a significant percentage of MPs and JPs. He entrusted reform to John Owen, the principal deviser of the scheme of triers and ejectors. In the time of Barebone's the very survival of the universities had come under powerful threat from radicals who condemned all worldly learning as a human and therefore popish adversary to God's truth and spirit. The protector characteristically disowned such thinking. By appointing Puritans as heads of colleges and as tutors, he and Owen secured the instillation of godly principles into their pupils. With the aim of spreading godly learning in the north, the protectorate also set in train the foundation of a new university at Durham, though the experiment withered.

In both religion and politics, he aimed to heal the breach between Presbyterians and Independents. Though the Independents had been his allies, he was always ready to accept Presbyterianism if it would only learn to tolerate godly dissenters from it. It was to his advantage that many clergy of the two denominations, demoralized on one side by the clamour of sectaries contemptuous of both of them, and encountering on the other the innate Anglicanism or inertia of the parishes, had begun to wonder whether their public feud over Church government might kill the Puritan cause.

Even so, ecumenical initiatives encountered obstinate resistance. So did Cromwell's exhortations towards Presbyterian tolerance.

Political Presbyterianism withstood him too. When, under the terms of the Instrument of Government, a parliament met in September 1654, he submitted the new constitution for its approval, only to encounter strenuous opposition from an alliance of commonwealthsmen and Presbyterians. He resorted to yet another military purge, forcibly excluding MPs who were unwilling to pledge a willingness to accept the Instrument even as a basis for political negotiation. The commonwealthsmen refused the test, but the Presbyterians stayed to fight. Though willing to accept a modified version of the Instrument, they insisted that the constitution could be legitimate only if its authority were declared to derive solely from parliament itself. No less than in 1642, MPs saw themselves as the ultimate arbiter of the nation's affairs. Cromwell, unwilling to yield on that principle, likewise would not agree to the practical revisions of the Instrument which the Presbyterians proposed. MPs insisted on tight restrictions on liberty of conscience and, again like their predecessors of 1642, challenged the ruler's control of the armed forces.

In January 1655, sooner than accept the parliament's terms, Cromwell dissolved it. In submitting the Instrument to it he had bidden for constitutional legitimacy. Now his power rested solely on the sword. The collection of non-parliamentary taxation was soon being challenged in the courts much as Charles I's had been. In March came a royalist rising. Charles II, having learned the lesson of his alliance with Presbyterians, had recently permitted only the network known as the Sealed Knot, which favoured the uncompromising royalist and Anglican stance of Hyde, to conspire within England on his behalf. But the Knot's lethargy and ineptitude persuaded the king to listen to other groups, who made contact with a number of Presbyterians and with disaffected groups in Cromwell's army, and whose wishful assessments of public support were smuggled across to the king. Their plans for a national rising collapsed. Only in Wiltshire, where the conspirators were led by the local gentleman John Penruddock, did the revolt get off the ground, and even there it was soon crushed.

Yet the regime, which exaggerated the royalist threat so as to scare parliamentarians into compliance with the protectorate, also feared it. In the wake of the rising the country was divided into twelve military zones, each with a Major-General at its head. Fourteen thousand royalists were required to give bonds for good behaviour; a register of royalist movements was kept; and, on the principle that the new measures had been necessitated by the intransigence of the king's party, the rule of the Major-Generals was financed by a 'decimation' tax laid on the Stuarts' past and present adherents, whether or not they had conspired against the protectorate. That transparent breach of the admittedly restricted amnesty which the Rump had granted in 1652 outraged not only royalists but many parliamentarians, who in the localities were starting to rebuild social bridges with their recent enemies.

Soon the duties of the Major-Generals were extended to the suppression of pleasures and sins that were held to have provoked God's wrath against the nation: to action against alehouses, maypoles, swearing, fornication, neglect of the Sabbath. Puritans of all persuasions had always favoured such policies, but only a handful of them welcomed the military methods that now enforced them. Though some

Major-Generals tried to work with JPs, the new system was essentially a substitute for local government and an acknowledgement of the government's inability to galvanize it.

The war on sin achieved few concrete results. Even as a security measure the Major-Generals had only short-term success. Cromwell hoped that they would train the county militia forces, to which the control of the regions could thus be increasingly trusted. In that way it would thus eventually be possible to wind down the standing army, which anyway had complied with a significant reduction since 1652. Yet the process was bound to be slow, for the army remained Cromwell's power base. In any case the militias were largely uncooperative. The truth was that the protectoral government, like the Rump and Barebone's before it, was isolated from the nation. Cromwell's efforts to broaden its appeal included the reduction of the monthly assessment to £60,000 a month, a step that might have been compatible with a peaceful foreign policy. His warlike one doomed his administration to a permanent and growing shortage of funds.

One economic expedient he contemplated was the legal readmission to England of the Jews, with their international commercial contacts and expertise. The Jewish community had been expelled in 1290, though a number of Jewish aliens were to be found in the capital who worshipped privately and unobtrusively – and who did not welcome the spotlight which Cromwell's proposal cast on them. Puritans were certain that Christ would come again only when the barrier between Jew and Gentile had been removed. Might it not, asked the protector, be the task of a Puritan ruler to advance that prospect? A conference called by him to discuss his proposal and its theological implications was predominantly hostile. He nonetheless secured the open toleration of the Jewish settlement, though legal endorsement came only after the Restoration.

Cromwell's foreign policy was a profound reversal of the Rump's. On becoming protector he concluded a treaty with the Dutch, though he declined to have the Navigation Act repealed and insisted on a secret clause in the treaty to exclude the House of Orange from power. His was the traditional aim of Puritanism: collaboration with Europe's other Protestant powers against their common Catholic enemies. Unfortunately those powers did not see themselves as natural allies either of England or of each other. Sweden, that rising Protestant force, which Cromwell wanted to attack the Habsburgs as it had done under Gustavus Adolphus, clashed with the Protestant Danes and Dutch over control of the Baltic, an arena of growing international consequence, not least as the source, on which England itself was dependent, of naval stores.

Still, Cromwell's army, and the navy that the Rump had built up, were powerful instruments of diplomacy. France and Spain were reduced to competing for his friendship. His target was Spain. Persuaded that the exhausted Spanish empire in the New World lay open to conquest, of which its wealth would more than meet the cost, he launched a combined military and naval expedition to the Caribbean to begin the process. Apparently invincible in his soldiering days, he was now humiliated. The expedition, appallingly organized and badly led, was a sorry contrast to the admittedly less ambitious expedition that Sir George Ayscue had taken to the New World in 1651–2. It was routed on Hispaniola (the island that today is shared by Haiti and the Dominican Republic) by a handful of Spanish settlers in April 1655. It limped on to Jamaica, which it did contrive to occupy, but the troops there were paralysed by sickness, division and despair. It was after hearing the news of Hispaniola, and ruminating on God's message in it, that Cromwell enlarged the responsibilities of the Major-Generals to encompass the war on sin.

The naval war spread to Europe, to the dismay of English traders to the Mediterranean. Blake did achieve an impressive victory off the Canary Islands in 1657. War with Spain meant alliance with France, which, so long as it took Spain for its enemy, could in Puritan eyes count as Protestant for diplomatic purposes. Even so, the French found Cromwell a tough negotiator. In 1655 he inflamed the talks by his protests over a massacre of Protestants in Piedmont by France's subordinate ally, the Duke of Savoy. In 1657, however, the Anglo-French alliance became closer. English troops joined French ones in Flanders in a campaign that in the following year would produce the English acquisition of Dunkirk. For the first time since the loss of Calais a century earlier, England had a territorial base across the Channel. One of Cromwell's conditions for an alliance with France had been the departure of Charles II from that country. In 1656 Charles was driven to sign a treaty with Spain in the unlikely hope of his restoration at that nation's hands. Spain's loss of Dunkirk to the English deprived him of that prospect. Yet the cost of the garrison proved unsustainable, and Charles II's government would sell it to the French in 1662.

The war against Spain disappointed two hopes of Cromwell: that it would rally the nation to his regime against England's long-standing traditional Catholic enemy, and that the costs of the conflict would be met by the seizure of Spanish ships and silver. The interruption of English trade to the Mediterranean provoked protests. By the summer of 1656 Cromwell's financial predicament was acute. Reluctantly he called another parliament, this one purged pre-emptively by orders forbidding around a hundred of the elected members to attend. Their removal, though a constitutional affront which offended the remaining members, worked. The assembly proved more cooperative than its predecessor of 1654–5. For the passage of time, and the failure of royalist conspiracy, had worked to the regime's advantage. Men who were too young to have known the passions behind the civil wars, and who were ready to accept any regime that would terminate the anarchy in which they had grown up, recognized the facts of power. Families which had withdrawn or been evicted from the running of the shires were returning to it. Parliament's mood arose not from any affection for the protector but from a determination to end military rule and restore a sense of normality.

Whereas the opponents of the army in the parliament of 1654 had antagonized Cromwell, their successors in the new parliament aimed to civilianize his rule – and thus tame it. Under the leadership of the Anglo-Irish grandee Lord Broghil, who had recently spent a year running the civilian administration of Scotland for Cromwell, they offered in the spring of 1657 to replace the Instrument of Government with another written constitution, formulated as the Humble Petition and Advice, which would steer England back towards the traditional monarchy, for whose abolition eight years earlier there had been so little support. Cromwell would be crowned king. There would be a second chamber of parliament, though, since the royalism of most of the peers precluded the restoration of the House of Lords, it would be replaced by an 'Other House', whose members the protector would nominate. Parliamentary restraints on the protector's powers would persist, but he would enjoy a greater degree of constitutional freedom than under the Instrument. From either realism or preference the supporters of the Humble Petition sought a Cromwellian rather than a Stuart monarchy. When Cromwellian rule collapsed two years later, their minds would turn to the alternative.

In anticipating the protector's liking for the new constitution of 1657, Broghil read the signs. Since 1653 as before it, Cromwell had striven to retain the allegiance of the two impulses which competed among England's rulers through the decade, and which under the protectorate vied with increasing acrimony inside and outside his entourage. Broghil himself, cautiously supported by John Thurloe, led the conservative tendency, which saw a Cromwellian dynasty as the practical solution to England's troubles. On the other side were those who, while they had been ready to accept Cromwell's rule as a unifying force against the Stuarts, or as an alternative to anarchy, or as the best means to secure liberty of conscience, did not want his enthronement or a return to old constitutional ways. That position was held by many of the people closest to him, some of them pliable civilians but others of them, who commanded much more influence, leading army officers. Chief among the latter were his son-in-law Charles Fleetwood, who had married Cromwell's daughter Bridget following the death in 1651 of her first husband, Ireton; and the protector's blunt-speaking brother-in-law John Desborough, a leading figure among the Major-Generals.

Over the course of the protectorate Cromwell gradually,

subtly, tilted the balance of power in favour of the conservatives. Among the naval commanders, sympathizers with commonwealthsmen found their influence diminished. At Oxford, John Owen, who opposed Broghil's stand, lost the Vice-Chancellorship, and yielded influence to John Wilkins, another brother-in-law of Cromwell, who supported it. In Scotland the military command of Robert Lilburne, whose political sympathies resembled Owen's, passed to George Monck, who favoured a return to monarchy. Plans which had been aired by radicals under the Rump for the transformation of Scottish legal and religious institutions, and for the breaking of the Scottish nobility, were moderated or dropped. Instead the Cromwellian council in Scotland concentrated on pragmatic and stabilizing reforms, on the balancing of parties among the clergy, and on the reconciliation of the Scots to English rule.

In Ireland, where Fleetwood was Lord Deputy, the shift of power was tortuously accomplished. Like much else in Cromwellian politics – as in monarchical politics before them – it was achieved after a power struggle within the ruling family. Fleetwood, to whom, both in England and among the civilian and military authorities in Ireland, opponents of the monarchical trend of the protectorate looked for leadership, was recalled to England in 1655. Yet he was incongruously allowed to retain his title while Henry Cromwell, the protector's second son and an ally of Broghil, ruled Ireland in his place. After two years of paralysing conflict between Henry's and Fleetwood's parties, Henry at last succeeded to the deputyship.

In England and Scotland the punishment of royalists had mostly extended only to their property or their pockets or their political rights. In Ireland a much harsher policy, laid down in legislation of 1652–3, prevailed. Hundreds of men were executed merely for having fought against the English parliament. Others were banished to the Caribbean, which had also become a dumping ground for vagabonds and royalist conspirators in England and Scotland. The centre-piece of the government's policy in Ireland was land confiscation. Perhaps getting on for half of the land there was seized from natives and taken over by English Protestants. Much of the territory was acquired by investors – 'Adventurers' – who had raised money for parliament to overcome the rising of 1641, and who now earned their returns. In 1652, when the Irish resistance had at last been subdued, the Rump began the process of reward. The English plantations that had been established since the early seventeenth century were to be extended by the carving up of the land of ten counties. Land not granted to Adventurers went to soldiers in the occupying army, of whom about 12,000 settled.

In a chaotic process, Catholic landowners were transplanted, under pain of death, to the western province of Connaught. Their tenants would have been transplanted too if the settlers had not realized that they needed them themselves, to work the land. The sternest advocates of retribution and transplantation were among Fleetwood's supporters, who viewed the Catholics as idolaters ripe for divine destruction. The same party was not much enamoured of the established Protestant settlers either. It saw conquered Ireland as a blank sheet, on which reforms of Church and law that were being resisted by interest groups in England could be inscribed. Baptists and other sects throve among the occupying soldiery and civilian administration. Henry Cromwell led the reaction. He gave encouragement to Presbyterianism and connived at the unofficial survival of episcopalian Protestantism. Such attempts as were made by the Cromwellians to win Irish Catholics to Protestantism wilted before the resentments which the occupation had intensified, though some converted in order to escape proscription.

When, in the spring of 1657, the Humble Petition and Advice was debated in the Commons and discussed with the protector, it was among Anglo-Irish Protestant MPs that it won its most significant support. The document offered his rule the constitutional sanction that he had failed to extract from the previous parliament. It also provided parliamentary endorsement, within limits with which he felt able to live, of liberty of conscience. He obliged the advocates of the Humble Petition by abandoning the rule of the Major-Generals. But would he accept the crown? As often before his great political decisions, he withdrew into himself. He prevaricated for weeks, seeking divine guidance and gauging the mood and power of the opponents of kingship in the army and congregations.

Among the officers, opposition presented a logical problem. The army leaders, after all, had offered Cromwell the crown in December 1653. How then could they object to his elevation now, save on the ground that the kingmakers were now their opponents? Fleetwood and Desborough reluctantly came round to the proposed new constitution, but there was a more formidable obstacle within the high command. John Lambert, twenty years Cromwell's junior, had been the architect of the Instrument of Government, and during the protectorate had been second only to Cromwell in political and military influence. A pragmatist, rarely touched by the visionary Puritanism of Cromwell's entourage, he seemed the one figure within the regime with both the political stature and the military base to succeed to the protectorate when, on Cromwell's death, the council chose his successor.

Yet Cromwell mistrusted him. The Humble Petition departed from the Instrument in providing for the present ruler to name his own successor. After Lambert had tried in vain to mobilize opposition to the new constitution, Cromwell made him resign his command and offices. Yet the protector, while accepting the bulk of the Humble Petition, defied general expectation by declining the crown. Historians have puzzled over his decision. Was it caused by the last-minute flurry of opposition which arose in the army and by fears for its unity? Or did the ageing and frequently ill Cromwell, on whom single rule had imposed high psychological strain, decide that God's will was against his further elevation, or else shirk the reproaches, and the renewed charges of self-seeking, that it would bring him from his own followers and in the wider nation? Or did he want to take the crown but decide that the time was not yet ripe to carry those supporters into acceptance?

Whatever the answer, his refusal was a bombshell. The debates over the Humble Petition had created a new political atmosphere. National settlement and stability had seemed within grasp, and the days of military rule had looked numbered. His decision, a symbolic triumph for the opponents of the conservative tendency, demoralized Broghil's party, many of whose members withdrew from parliament in disgust, so that the Humble Petition, now without the kingly title, only scraped through the Commons before the parliament was adjourned. Cromwell was reinstalled as protector in June 1657, in a ceremony whose stately grandeur stood in contrast to his plain inauguration in 1653. He was king in all but name. Yet the occasion which raised him to that height was also the moment when the protectorate, and with it Puritan rule, began to unravel.

5

RESTORATION

❧·❦

If the protector had accepted the crown in 1657, and been ready to face down the military opponents of his elevation, perhaps a Cromwellian dynasty would have endured. Such an outcome of the civil wars would have been inconceivable in 1642. If it had happened, however, at least the wars would have produced, by the lights of those who had contended against Charles I, some gains. A Puritan monarchy would have replaced a Laudian one, while some of the restraints imposed on the protector by the Humble Petition and Advice echoed Pym's proposals for the limitation of the crown's powers in 1641–2.

Under the new constitution the monarchical trend continued. There was talk of calling a new parliament and of reviving the move to crown Cromwell. His son Richard was given tasks to prepare him for rule and was brought on to the executive council, which was now given the regal title of 'privy council', and whose members, as under the monarchy, were 'their lordships'. Yet the kingship party was doggedly opposed by the newly heartened Fleetwood and Desborough, their brief readiness to swallow Cromwell's enthronement forgotten. Lambert's administrative abilities and political adroitness were missed. By now the protector's balancing act could produce only stalemate. As his health declined in 1658, his government, which had always struggled, with a small staff, to keep up with the problems of running three divided kingdoms, more or less ground to a halt.

Political disaster struck in early 1658 with the recall of the parliament that had passed the Humble Petition. The MPs who had been excluded from its first session were allowed back, and used wrecking tactics. The 'Other House' was a fiasco. The protector had welcomed it as a balance to the Commons' powers, and particularly to its instinctive intolerance. But those of the existing peers whom he invited to join the new chamber refused. The low social origins of the Cromwellian officers who did agree to sit, and who called themselves 'lords', were treated disdainfully by the Commons. After two barren weeks the protector, alarmed by a revival of discontent in the army and the City, dissolved the parliament in something like panic.

He died on 3 September 1658, the anniversary of his victories at Dunbar and Worcester. He had characteristically kept men guessing about the succession, but councillors who had gathered at his deathbed maintained that, in a lucid interval of his fevered state, he had indicated that Richard should follow him. A gentle and insubstantial figure, with no personal authority in the army, Richard seemed to some a more acceptable candidate for kingship than his father. He at least would not lead military coups against parliament. Unfortunately the army, knowing his sympathies to be with Broghil and the kingship party, was soon ready to act without him. Fleetwood, who took over the leadership of the army, lacked Oliver's stature within it. Mounting arrears of pay fuelled discontent, especially among the junior officers, who revived the practices of organization and protest on which the Levellers had thrived in 1647. They tugged Fleetwood and Desborough into confrontation with Richard and the kingship party.

They were no less hostile to the parliament which Richard summoned in January 1659, and which, like other parliaments over the past twelve years, demanded the cessation of political agitation among the soldiery. Soon Fleetwood and Richard were openly competing for the allegiance of the forces. Fleetwood prevailed, and at his and Desborough's insistence Richard dissolved the parliament on 22 April. Richard himself, after a tussle with the commonwealthsmen, was forced into abdication in early May. The protectorate was over.

How would it be replaced? The army, knowing no way forward, went backward. Again suspending its differences with the civilian commonwealthsmen, it restored the Rump, which it had expelled in 1653. Enemies of the house of Cromwell, in their joy at its fall, used the vague slogan 'the good old cause' to disguise the bankruptcy of their constitutional thinking from the world and from themselves. Commonwealthsmen in the Rump maintained that legally they had held power all along, and that Cromwellian rule had merely 'interrupted' their sovereignty. Yet sooner or later the electorate which the Rump claimed to represent would have to be consulted. The parliament promised to dissolve itself within a year, but the old quandary raised by that prospect set MP against MP, army officer against army officer.

One party, intemperately led in the Commons by Sir Arthur Hesilrige, maintained a simple belief in the undivided sovereignty of the Commons, a principle which, its adherents persuaded themselves, would have won acceptance by the nation if Cromwell had not foreshortened its implementation in 1653. The other party followed the thinking that had led Cromwell himself to welcome the 'Other House'. That experiment had perished with the protectorate, but Sir Henry Vane and others wanted the formation of a 'senate', nominated rather than elected, which would check any counter-revolutionary tendencies in the elected Commons and would preserve the political and religious principles of the good old cause. The idea found favour in the army, where officers saw in it, as they had in the 'Other House', a means to the entrenchment of their own influence.

Neither solution would have commended itself to the electorate. The summer produced a major rising, led by the former Presbyterian MP Sir George Booth in Cheshire, which brought Presbyterians and royalists together. It was crushed by Lambert, who had been restored to his command after the fall of the protectorate. His triumph reignited his political ambitions. The man who had ended parliamentary sovereignty by framing the Instrument of Government was no friend to that principle now. In October he secured the second forcible expulsion of the Rump. The cause, once again, was the clash of military and civilian. Hesilrige, treating the army with a contempt as keen as that vented on it by Denzil Holles twelve years earlier, had incited the Rump to the settling of scores. It purged officers who had supported the protectorate; it demanded the army's unqualified submission to the Commons; and it strove to win officers and men over to its cause. Yet the army, having redissolved the Rump in retaliation, again knew no way forward. The best it could manage was the appointment of an ad hoc Committee of Safety. Some members of the Rump agreed to serve on it alongside army officers, but its claims to power were widely resisted or ignored.

At least the Rump had represented, however imperfectly, civilian and parliamentary authority. Its second eviction began the slide to the Restoration. The law courts closed; discontent mounted in the City, where soldiers were hooted with derision; and the onset of a tax strike threatened to cripple the army. Londoners, themselves victims of a trading depression, voiced the demand, which in the ensuing months became a national cry, for a full and free parliament. Everyone knew what that meant. Parliamentary and military and protectoral rule having all discredited and destroyed themselves, a free parliament would restore the Stuart line.

By December the Committee of Safety and the army leadership were in disarray. Regiments defected to the commonwealthsmen; the navy was secured for them too; and Hesilrige prepared to lead troops on London from Portsmouth. In desperation, senior officers thought briefly of inviting the king back themselves, sooner than risk his restoration at the hands of their opponents. Instead, at the end of the year, they brought back the Rump for its third, briefest, tenure. Hopeless as both its and the army's cause might seem, between them they did command the troops, whose existence remained a seemingly insuperable obstacle to the monarchy's return.

It was the conduct of the commander of the forces in Scotland, George Monck, that enabled the Restoration to be accomplished without bloodshed. He had weeded commonwealthsmen and sectaries from the regiments north of the border, and had forged a disciplined and united force. Though no friend to republican rule, he was shocked by the coup of October 1659, and he opposed the subsequent military takeover. Lambert led forces north to confront him, but they crumbled away. In January Monck brought his army into England, ostensibly in support of the Rump, which trusted to his professions of friendship. First invisibly, then transparently, he plotted its overthrow. In February he surprised it by escorting into the Commons a large body of MPs who had ceased to sit at Pride's Purge, and who now, as before the purge, commanded a Presbyterian majority. With pardonable exaggeration a royalist wryly observed that there had come to be 'more governments on foot than all Europe has had for centuries of years'.

The more of them there were, the likelier became the return of the Stuart monarchy. But what form would the Restoration take? In the later 1640s the Presbyterians had sought to impose on a defeated and captive king the conditions for the return of monarchy. Now they hoped to impose comparable terms on an exiled one. Their expectation of a Presbyterian future was evident too in their vote to resurrect the Church settlement that had been stillborn in the 1640s. With Monck's blessing they arranged the general parliamentary elections that the Rump and army alike had feared. Thus the Long Parliament, which by the statute of 1641 could not be dissolved without its own consent, had at last given it. It also resolved to restore the House of Lords. Elections were held in April, and the members whom they returned met on the 25th. By that time Monck had sent an emissary to the king in Holland. In deference to Charles, without whom no parliament could be legally summoned, the members of the new body called it a 'Convention', but the assembly commanded a wider basis of support than any that had claimed to be a parliament since 1641.

The Presbyterian and royalist parties in the Convention seem to have been equally balanced. Yet Presbyterian hopes were swept away by a tide of national feeling. The roasting of rumps in the streets, the erection of maypoles, the open celebration of Easter, all testified to a sense of emancipation, which turned against every form of parliamentarian and Puritan rule. In 1648 resurgent royalism and Anglicanism had been crushed by the new model army. In 1660 the same army, demoralized, divided, desperate for its arrears, accepted Monck as its commander-in-chief and gave up its cause. Part of it would be taken over by the crown after the Restoration, when the rest would disband without resistance.

In Ireland, coup and counter-coup in 1659–60 left both the Cromwellians and the commonwealthsmen powerless. The English navy went over to Charles, as part of it had done in 1648. Though Puritanism was strong in the fleet, and though anti-monarchical feeling had flourished there as a result of the purge of the officers in 1649, the navy was a pliable force, which had adjusted to the coups of 1653 and which now adjusted to the Restoration. Monck's counterpart in its leadership was Pepys's patron Edward Montagu, a former new model soldier who had disowned his early religious radicalism, had become a conservative councillor under Cromwell, and would thrive, as the Earl of Sandwich, in the Restoration.

Even when the Convention met, conditions might still have been imposed on the king's return. Monck himself feared the sway of extreme royalism that an unconditional restoration might produce. It was Charles who undermined the Presbyterians, by issuing at Breda a declaration which reached Westminster shortly after the Convention had assembled. It committed the king to responding sympathetically to whatever proposals parliament might make for the paying off of the soldiers and for the disposition of property confiscated during the wars. There were to be liberty of conscience and a general pardon, within limits which parliament itself would determine.

Since the declaration, which cleverly shifted on to parliament the burden of settling the main post-war problems, appeared to guarantee the spirit of parliamentary monarchy, the Presbyterian demand for the letter of it looked gracelessly superfluous. On 1 May the two Houses voted to restore government 'by King, Lords and Commons'. Charles promptly sailed, in a fleet sent over by parliament and led by Montagu, for Dover, where a great crowd awaited him. At its head was Monck, whom the king in gratitude raised from his knees, and whom he would make a duke in reward for steering through the Restoration. The king's return to London and his coronation were greeted by bonfires, bell-ringing, ecstatic acclamations, and a great deal of public drinking. The two decades that had turned the worlds of politics and religion upside down were past.

Viewed in retrospect, the year 1660 is one of the clear dividing lines of English history, in company with 1066, 1485, and 1832. Yet the rejoicing which accompanied the return of the crown, and which the king himself viewed with fitting scepticism, obscured the uncertainty of the political future. By 1667 the restored regime was in trouble. In that year the flight into exile of Clarendon, the king's leading minister, to avoid parliamentary impeachment recalled the rout of Charles I's advisers in 1640–1. It followed the unopposed advance up the Medway of Dutch ships which set fire to English ones, a humiliation quite as bitter as the fiascos of Charles I's military expeditions in the 1620s. People, noticed Pepys, were now nostalgic for the rule of 'Oliver', who had 'made all the neighbour princes fear him'. There was greater instability in the 1670s, when the prospect of Charles's succession by his Catholic brother James revived the fear and hatred of popery, and provoked the parliamentary battles from which the Whig and Tory parties, heirs to the parliamentarian and royalist ones, emerged.

For the tensions that had led to civil war, far from being resolved by them, had been entrenched by the antagonisms they bequeathed. The conflict of 1640–60, by polarizing the nation, bequeathed habits of polarized thinking. By the later part of Charles II's reign, theories of royal absolutism, and on the other side arguments for the accountability of kings to their subjects, confronted each other with a directness that had rarely been known before 1640. Yet if the conflict of crown and parliament persisted, it took different forms. Charles II, flexible, pragmatic, loose in manners and morals, may have done nothing for the dignity of kingship, but at least he did not repeat his father's mistakes. He explained that religious toleration, which both in Laudian and in mainstream Puritan eyes was an enemy to civil peace, had become essential to it and to national reconciliation. Instead of tying the crown, as Charles I had done, to an intolerant and narrowly based Church, he set Anglicans, Catholics and Puritans against each other, and in the process asserted the right of the crown to exempt religious groups from statutory restraints on their worship.

In politics, too, he took a broad-based approach, to the mortification of former royalists who expected a monopoly of power in compensation for their loyal sufferings. Former parliamentarians who had opposed the regicide were indulgently treated. The perpetrators of that deed were another matter. A number of the regicides were dragged through the streets past jeering spectators to be hanged, drawn and quartered, a plight which others evaded only by escaping into exile. Cromwell's corpse was exhumed and, on the twelfth anniversary of the regicide, derisively hanged and decapitated at Tyburn.

In the reaction against Puritan and parliamentarian rule, the reforms which it had enacted were swept from the record. Even the redistribution of parliamentary constituencies, which rectified what was widely agreed to be a scandal, was forgotten in the almost instinctive return to old constitutional ways. The only legislative legacy of the two decades from 1640 lay in the laws to which the king had consented in 1641. It was a thin one. The restored regime found the most significant constitutional change of that year, the Triennial Act, all too significant. It was replaced in 1664 by a less stringent triennial law, which left the initiative for calling parliaments solely to the king, and which Charles II was able to ignore with impunity in the last years of his reign. The prerogative courts of Star Chamber and High Commission, which had been used or abused to implement the contentious policies of the 1630s, were permanently removed. A small number of measures passed in the years after 1641 were preserved, in whole or in part, by new ones, which silently passed over their debt to the Roundhead initiatives. One of them was the abolition of the Court of Wards in 1646, another the Navigation Act of 1651. But no one would have undergone the civil wars for the sake of that legislative yield.

It has often been said that the execution of Charles I was

a salutary lesson to his successors, and that the monarchy was wary of overexerting its prerogatives thereafter. It did not look that way in the last years of Charles II's reign or, after Charles's death in 1685, for most of James II's brief one. Like the Cromwellian regime before it, the restored government both feared and exaggerated the risk from conspiracy, at home and abroad, by the defeated party. The danger gave a pretext for the crown's gradual accumulation of a standing army, which Charles I had lacked, and which, by the time James II had expanded it, was comparable in size to the new model. James himself developed techniques of electoral manipulation which confined membership of the Commons to his supporters.

In 1688 the crisis of 1640–2 repeated itself. Again constitutional anxieties mingled with the fear of popery. In 1640 leading peers had conspired with the Scots to bring down the non-parliamentary rule of Charles I. In 1688 leading peers conspired with William of Orange to drive James II into abdication. If the first emergency produced twenty years of chaos and the second was swiftly resolved, there are two reasons for the contrast. The dissidents of 1688 found in William and his wife Mary, James's daughter, what their predecessors of 1640 had lacked, an alternative candidacy for the throne; and James, unlike his father, did not hold his nerve and fight.

By contrast the politics of the eighteenth century would be relatively stable – until, towards its end, the rise of popular radicalism created the next set of explosive issues. It was the revolution of 1688–9 and its aftermath, not the civil wars, that achieved the relative stability. William's reign effected the peaceable alteration in the balance of crown and parliament that had eluded John Pym and his colleagues. The change came from two sources: the readiness of the king, who had annexed England for the purposes of Dutch foreign policy, to trade constitutional powers for the parliamentary revenue with which to fight France, now the common enemy of England and the Netherlands and the ally of the deposed Stuarts; and, in the years around the foundation of the Bank of England in 1694, a revolution in state finance that tied government borrowing to parliamentary revenue and thus to the holding of parliaments. Since 1689 there has been a parliament in session every year.

Across the turning point of 1688, however, there ran long-term tendencies for which the first as well as the second of the upheavals of the seventeenth century bears responsibility. They do not entitle us to call the civil wars a 'revolution' of the kind which, in France and Russia – and in the American War of Independence – would transform, and be intended to transform, perceptions of the nature of politics or of liberty. Yet the wars, together with the convulsion of 1688, did have transforming effects, albeit inadvertent ones.

For wars, civil or foreign, have to be won, and the winning of them requires money and power. The civil wars doubled the proportion of national income commanded by the state, and the wars fought by William to defend his regime in the 1690s would double it again. Both the army which defeated Charles I, and the navy of the 1650s, would cost the taxpayer about twice as much a year as the total annual income of Queen Elizabeth. Government income in 1700 seems to have been about ten times as high as in 1600. It is an ironic achievement of the resistance to Charles I that it helped to solve the problem which the king had striven to overcome, the underfinancing of government. From the expansion of state revenue there would be built the army and navy that enabled England to become an imperial power.

Here for once results bore some relation to intentions, for the diplomatic and economic ambitions of the regimes of the 1650s were meant to make the nation mighty. If Cromwell had not ended the Dutch war, claimed Thomas Scot, the MP who was one of its architects, the English might have become 'masters of the whole world'. But it was trade, not imperial territory, that the war was meant to win. Cromwell did have territorial ambitions in Spanish America. Yet when the abject forces which he sent to the Caribbean acquired Jamaica, his sole lasting acquisition for England, it was the destruction of Antichrist, not the creation of the British Empire, that he had in mind.

There was a second ironic outcome of the civil wars. Before them the apparatus of government, and the patronage at its command, had been small by Continental standards, and too small to make the reforms of Charles I effective. The swelling of the state's resources and administration to meet the demands of war in the 1640s and 1650s, and then again in the 1690s, resolved that problem. Like the enhancement of government revenue it provoked loud but impotent protests. During the civil wars we find the first statements of a demand which by the end of the century became a movement, for the disqualification of government employees – 'placemen' as they came to be called – from membership of the Commons, whose independence their presence was deemed to be eroding. Whereas the seventeenth century quarrelled about the rights of parliament in relation to the monarchy, the eighteenth would be exercised by the shared power of monarch and parliament – the state – over the nation. The subject's liberties came to seem threatened less by the royal prerogative, which was the preoccupation of Stuart politics, than by the corruption that was alleged to thrive on the expansion of patronage, which was the preoccupation of Hanoverian ones. The testing of the royal prerogative destabilized the first era: patronage helped stabilize, even as it soured, the second.

In 1660 the religious future, like the political one, was open. The likeliest outcome, favoured by Charles, seemed to be an accommodation between Anglicanism and the more moderate Puritans, especially those among the Presbyterians. There was, admittedly, intense opposition to the idea among Anglicans, especially among churchmen who in the civil wars had been driven from their livings and had subsequently been steadfast under persecution, using the Anglican liturgy in private and sustaining its lay devotees. Many younger men, defying Puritan regulations, had been secretly and defiantly ordained under the pre-war procedures. Theologians, Henry Hammond at their head, had also helped to preserve the distinctive identity of Anglicanism. They produced treatises which, in their calm and rational and practical spirit and in their insistence that salvation is open to all, commanded a wider appeal than the theological convolutions and the predestinarianism of Puritanism ever could.

Yet there were also large numbers of Anglican churchmen who had compromised with the Puritan ascendancy in order to acquire or retain their livings. They were likewise ready to compromise with Presbyterianism in 1660, when negotiations over Church government and the Prayer Book were held between leaders of the Anglican and Presbyterian denominations. The talks were plagued by intransigence, but what doomed them was the meeting of the 'Cavalier Parliament', which replaced the Convention in 1661. It was in the elections to it that the scale of the national reaction against Puritan rule was revealed. The influence which the Presbyterians had commanded in the Convention was sharply reduced.

Presbyterianism, which can claim to have been the political and ecclesiastical mainstream of the Puritan movement in the civil war, was the great loser of the conflict, caught as it was between royalism on one side and radicalism on the other. In the late 1640s it was thwarted by the army. In the early 1660s it was seen off by the resurgence of royalism and Anglicanism, and was left to share the defeat of the other Puritan groups, whose enemy it had been. Parliament, which in the 1640s had abolished episcopacy, from 1661 loyally subscribed to the principle of James I, 'No bishop, no king'. In 1662 the Act of Uniformity, which required the clergy to pledge undeviating adherence to the Prayer Book, led to the eviction of thousands of ministers. A series of other measures in the 1660s penalized the worship of Puritans or, as they came to be called, Dissenters or Nonconformists, and forbade them to hold national or local office. Although the legislation was unevenly enforced, it led to widespread imprisonment and suffering.

Of all the outcomes of the civil wars, none had more enduring consequences than the Anglican legislation that followed them. Its legacy, prolonged by the Toleration Act of 1689, which, though it gave Dissenters religious rights, denied them civil ones, was the split in national culture that, in later ages, became the divide of Church and chapel and, with it, of Tory and Liberal. Under the later Stuarts the restored Church was wise in its generation, making common cause with parliamentarian intolerance when the crown offered inducements, as it had done in the civil wars, to Catholics and Puritans. Instead of sinking with the monarchy, as in 1640, the Church was able, in 1688, to stand for the nation against it.

The Restoration left Puritanism to lick its self-inflicted wounds. Puritans who had believed themselves to be fighting for God's cause blamed each other for destroying it. Instead of converting and purifying the world, the hope which the civil wars had brought them, they now had to concentrate, as in the 1630s, on their survival in it. How had the divine favour which had awarded them their victories deserted them? In 1649 Henry Hammond had said on behalf of royalism that in permitting the regicide God 'hath spat in our face'. Now the tables were turned. 'The Lord', lamented Charles Fleetwood as the disintegration of the Puritan cause began in 1659, had 'spat in the faces' of his followers. The God who had answered parliamentarian prayers now answered royalist ones. 'The court of heaven', declared a future bishop in 1660, 'hath been solicited this many years *pro* and *con* ... and now let the world judge whose prayers have been answered.'

The abasement and agony of the Puritans' defeat, and their struggle to make sense of their reverse, are immortalized by analogy in *Samson Agonistes*, one of the great late poems of the blind Milton, who with the fall of Puritanism had returned from prose to verse. Though some Dissenters conspired against the restored regime, most submitted to the judgement of providence. They sought, by demonstrating their peaceable intent, to persuade the crown to grant them liberty of worship. Much of the energy of Dissent, excluded from politics, turned to trade and to the pursuit of respectability through it. Radical sects of the 1650s, the Quakers among them, gradually became respectable too. John Bunyan, a militant sectary in the civil wars, suffered imprisonment after the Restoration. His *The Pilgrim's Progress*, published in 1678, was written with polemical intent. Yet in its travel down the centuries its metaphor for the inner struggle of the godly soul lost its subversive tinge. Its sober vision is a world away from the dissolute court of Charles II, from its wits and rakes and blasphemers, and from the laughter of the Restoration stage.

If the civil wars bequeathed the triumph of Anglicans and the humiliation of Puritans, they also fostered developments that distressed both parties. The causes of historical movements are never self-contained. There were intellectual and social tendencies of the later seventeenth century which can be explained as reactions against the civil wars, but which also belonged to long-term movements of ideas that were as much European as English. Calvinism, in England and outside it, can be seen in retrospect to have gone against the grain of a century in which the foundations of biblical certainty were gradually undermined, and in which the scope of man's reason to understand the world, and the power of his free will to improve it, were acknowledged with ever fewer inhibitions. England at the end of the seventeenth century was not, as far as can be judged, a less devout society than it had been fifty years earlier, but it had less use for theological intricacy, more interest in Christianity as an aid to moral and sociable life. By the end of the century even the Dissenters' God had lost some of his Old Testament terror.

The lasting intellectual consequences of the civil wars were those which turned against, or stood back from, the passions that had animated the conflict. Inquiries of the mind – thanks in some cases to royalists who returned from exile abreast of Continental thinking – had ever more to do with the observation of man and the world as they are, and ever less with how zealots, whether Puritan or Anglican, said they ought to be. The Royal Society, founded in 1662, was largely shaped by scientists who had held high posts in Cromwellian Oxford. There, however, they had pleaded for empirical investigation, free from the dogmatism and the party allegiances of the rulers of the university. One of the initial Fellows was William Petty, the pioneer of political economy, whose land survey of Ireland in the 1650s, designed to bring order to the Cromwellian allocation of property there, was among the incidental advances in political and social analysis that were produced, not in pursuit of the goals of the civil wars, but by the chaos that they wrought.

So was *The Commonwealth of Oceana*, a treatise of 1656 by the political thinker James Harrington, which explained the recent breakdown of English politics, not as a confrontation of ideologies, but as a product of alterations in the patterns of property holding that had weakened the crown in relation to the landowners. His thesis, which has had its modern imitators, was flawed, but his conception of the relationship of power to property would be taken up by David Hume and other pioneers of sociology in the next century. With other thinkers, Harrington insisted that political health and stability rest on an understanding of men's legitimate and competing interests. Like Thomas Hobbes, he maintained that protestations of godliness, which had been the motor of the civil wars, masked worldly motives.

In religious as in political thinking there is a distance, if not opposition, between the consequences of the wars and the purposes of their participants. Arguments for religious toleration won widening support in the later seventeenth century, but not because of the spiritual arguments which

Congregationalists and sectaries of the civil wars had advanced on behalf of freedom of conscience. It was rather because the ecclesiastical disorder of those decades had made religious pluralism a fact of life, which advocates of tolerance now judged likelier than intolerance to reconcile with society's requirements of peace and prosperity. Anglicans and Puritans alike were disheartened by the long-term secularizing trend of political and intellectual debate. It had defied their efforts, in the first case in the 1630s, in the second during the 1640s and 1650s, to impose a partisan religious vision on politics and society. It was still more potent now.

Historic events have two lives, the first experienced by those who live through them, the second by those who remember them and who find reflections of their own preoccupations in them. Successive generations have selectively interpreted the civil wars to the advantage of their own causes. Until the nineteenth century, royalist sympathizers had the better of the argument. As Hobbes observed after the Restoration, 'there can be nothing more instructive towards loyalty ... than will be the memory, while it lasts, of the civil wars.' It lasted long, even if the effusiveness of royalist sympathizers was slowly modified as theories of divine-right kingship receded.

In the later seventeenth and the early eighteenth centuries the clash of Whig and Tory throve on the publication of memoirs and documentary collections recording the wars. A few brave defenders of the regicide survived into the eighteenth century, to the embarrassment of orthodox Whigs, who preferred to forget the wars and to portray the swift and aristocratic coup of 1688–9, which had brought them to power, as the foundation of modern liberty. Their discomfort was exposed by Anglicans, who took advantage, in zealous sermons, of the stipulation made by the Prayer Book of 1662 for the condemnation of the regicide in services to be held on its every anniversary, a provision that was not repealed for two centuries. Whigs were no less troubled to recall the religious fanaticism of the Puritan cause, which they tried to write out of the record.

In the nineteenth century the picture changed. The religious revival of the era, and the alliance of the expanding and newly confident movement of Nonconformity with the Liberal Party, inspired the recovery of the Puritan past, in which Dissent now celebrated its ancestry. Hitherto the character of Oliver Cromwell, on which partisan perceptions of the war have always tended to focus, had been generally demonized even when his diplomatic exploits had been admired. But he became a cult figure among Victorians, who after a long controversy raised a statute to him at Westminster in 1899. He was hailed not only for his religion but, in another exercise of selectivity, as the friend of the middle and lower classes against aristocratic oppression. On the same principle the aristocratic character of the Glorious Revolution now made it seem the inferior, not the superior, of the earlier transformation.

The notion that Cromwell, whose troops successively broke up the House of Commons, and who turned to and against parliaments solely as he could use them to further God's cause, was a friend to parliamentary 'democracy', a pejorative word in his circle, is still with us. Victorian Chartists and republicans made a hero of him, though by the end of the century socialists were discovering the virtues of the Levellers, a group whose social programme had been forgotten since 1660, and were condemning his 'capitalist' suppression of them. There has also been Cromwell as a precursor, generally reviled, sometimes admired, of Napoleon or even Hitler. Yet the transformation he sought was religious, not political. When set, not only against those later dictators, but beside the most ambitious rulers of his own century – Gustavus Adolphus, the Great Elector of Brandenburg, Louis XIV – he does not look a state builder.

The recruitment of the passions of the civil wars by later causes has sustained the public interest in the period. But it has also distorted the conflict and has sometimes romanticized it. When the passions subsided, what goals of the participants had they profited? Royalists at least regained the throne which their king had needlessly lost. But the parliamentarians who defeated him and demolished the nation's institutions, and whose exploits were swiftly and emphatically reversed in 1660, would have had no persuasive answer to a poem of 1700 by John Dryden, in which the writer's fancy delivered an address to the departing century and contemplated the conflict of its central decades. He had walked, with Milton and Marvell, in Cromwell's funeral procession. The years had made him a Tory and Jacobite, but there is more wisdom than disdain in his assessment: 'Thy wars brought nothing about.'

CHRONOLOGY OF MAIN EVENTS

❧·❧

Apr.–May 1640	Short Parliament
Nov. 1640	Long Parliament meets
May 1641	Execution of Strafford
Oct. 1641	Irish Rebellion breaks out
Nov. 1641	Grand Remonstrance passed
Jan. 1642	Attempt to arrest the five members; the king leaves London
Aug. 1642	Charles raises standard at Nottingham
Oct. 1642	Battle of Edgehill
Sep. 1643	Solemn League and Covenant
July 1644	Battle of Marston Moor
Feb. 1645	Legislation for new model army passed
June 1645	Battle of Naseby
May 1646	Charles surrenders to Scots; fall of Oxford
Feb. 1647	Charles handed over to parliament
June 1647	Charles taken into army's custody; army's march on London
July 1647	Heads of Proposals drawn up
Apr.–Sep. 1648	Second Civil War
Dec. 1648	Pride's Purge
Jan. 1649	Charles tried and executed
Mar. 1649	Abolition of House of Lords

May 1649	Levellers suppressed; England declared a Commonwealth
Sep.–Oct. 1649	Battles of Drogheda and Wexford
Sep. 1650	Battle of Dunbar
Sep. 1651	Battle of Worcester
Apr. 1653	Expulsion of Long Parliament
July–Dec. 1653	Barebone's Parliament
Dec. 1653	Instrument of Government; Cromwell becomes Lord Protector
Sep. 1654–Jan. 1655	First protectorate parliament
Aug.–Oct. 1655	Rule of Major-Generals institutionalized
Sep. 1656–Feb. 1658	Second protectorate parliament
June 1657	Implementation of Humble Petition and Advice
Sep. 1658	Death of Cromwell; son Richard succeeds
Jan.–Apr. 1659	Richard Cromwell's parliament
May 1659–Feb. 1660	Intermittent rule of restored Rump of Long Parliament
Jan. 1660	Monck marches into England
Feb. 1660	MPs purged in Dec. 1648 restored
Apr. 1660	Election of Convention
May 1660	Charles II restored

FURTHER READING

❧·❦

In the decades around 1900 the documentary enquiries and ambitious narratives of S. R. Gardiner and C. H. Firth gave foundations to the study of the civil wars which have not been matched for the surrounding periods, and from which the modern scholarly preoccupation with the subject arose. There would be no difficulty in filling the space of this book with a list of valuable publications which have appeared in the subsequent century or so, especially in the second half of it. The best starting point is Austin Woolrych's magisterial survey *Britain in Revolution 1625–1660* (2002), which contains careful guidance on the recent literature – in which further pointers can in turn be found. Of the cascade of scholarly books to have appeared even since Woolrych's was completed, perhaps those most rewarding to the general reader are John Adamson, *The Noble Revolt: The Overthrow of Charles I* (2007), which emphasizes the role of the aristocracy in the events of 1640–2; John Barratt, *Cavaliers: The Royalist Army at War* (2000); Barry Coward, *The Cromwellian Protectorate* (2002); David Cressy, *England on Edge: Crisis and Revolution 1640–1642* (2006), which centres on popular discontent and disturbances; Richard Cust, *Charles I: A Political Life* (2005); Ian Gentles's textbook *The English Revolution and the Wars in the Three Kingdoms 1638–1652* (2007); James R. Hart's account of legal and constitututional issues, *The Rule of Law 1603–1660* (2003); Clive Holmes's collection of essays, broader in scope than its title suggests, *Why was Charles I Executed?* (2006), to which the reader wanting a shorter account than Woolrych's might turn first; Neil Keeble, *The Restoration: England in the 1660s* (2002); Jason McElligott and David Smith (eds), *Royalists and Royalism during the English Civil Wars* (2007), another collection of essays; Carla Gardiner Pestana's study of the American colonies, *The English Atlantic in an Age of Revolution 1640–1661* (2007); Trevor Royle's narrative account, *Civil War: The Wars of the Three Kingdoms 1638–1660;* and David Scott's more analytical treatment, *Politics and War in the Three Stuart Kingdoms, 1637–49* (2004), which like Gentles's textbook gives full weight to the conflicts in Ireland and Scotland.

The most influential and stimulating historian of the 1640s and 1650s in recent times has been John Morrill, whose collection of essays *The Nature of the English Revolution* (1993) remains an indispensable introduction to recent debates about the period. Woolrych might have made more use of three books with substantial discussions of the fiscal or commercial dimensions of the wars: Michael Braddick, *Parliamentarian Taxation in Seventeenth-Century England* (1994); Robert Brenner, *Merchants and Revolution* (1993); and James Scott Wheeler, *The Making of a World Power* (1999). I have discussed perceptions of the wars from their own time to the modern age in my *Roundhead Reputations: The English Civil Wars and the Passions of Posterity* (2001), and the literary dimension of the conflict in my *Literature and Politics in Cromwellian England: John Milton, Andrew Marvell, Marchamont Nedham* (2007). Two excellent books, both concerned with the 1640s, have appeared since this volume was written:

Michael Braddick, *God's Fury, England's Fire* (2008), which is particularly strong on the social conflicts of the era and their reflection in the pamphlet literature of the time; and Barbara Donagan, *War in England 1642–1649* (2008), which centres on the values and conduct of the soldiers. At the last moment let me add the collection of essays edited by Jenny Wormald, *The Seventeenth Century* (2008), another study to integrate English with British developments.

INDEX

❦

Act of Uniformity (1662), 159
adultery, condemned, 115
Africa, naval expedition to, 107
Agreements of the People (1647, 1649), army documents, 101, 106
alehouses, suppressed, 134
altars, and ecclesiastical policies, 24, 44
American colonies, 107, 119, 121–2, 169; *see also* New England
American War of Independence, 156
Anglicans, Anglicanism: and Reformation, 9, 11–12; beliefs and doctrines, 11–12, 44; church buildings, 12; and foreign policy, 13; and first civil war, 50; and second civil war, 96; from Restoration, 112, 153, 158–9, 159–60, 161, 164; and protectorate, 130–31; liturgy, 158; and secularization, 163; *see also* Arminianism; Prayer Book

Anglo-Dutch wars: (1652–4), 120, 122–3, 136, 157; (1665–7), 152–3
Anglo-Spanish wars: (1585–1604), 3, 13; (1655–60), 136–8, 157
Argyll, Archibald Campbell, 1st Marquis of, Scottish Presbyterian magnate, 59, 86
aristocracy *see* peers
Arminianism, doctrine of free will, 20, 21–2, 31–2, 35, 80
Arminius, Jacobus, Dutch divine, 20
army (English): reform of (Charles I), 6; costs of, 18, 30, 32; ill-discipline of, 28; disbanding of, 38; militia ordinance (1642), 40, 62; under Charles II and James II, 155
armies (parliamentarian): raising and recruitment of, 46, 53–4, 56, 59, 62, 73; promotions, 54–5; reorganization (1644–5), 61, 84–5; size, 62, 72–3; mutinous, 87; *see also* Ironsides; new model army; officers

173